Children Becoming Readers

Related titles from Macmillan Education

Assessment: From Principles to Action
Robin Lloyd-Jones and Elizabeth Bray

Reading: Guides to Assessment in Education
Bridie Raban

Resources for Reading: Does Quality Count?
UKRA Conference Proceedings, 1985: Editor, Betty Root

Assessing Reading
UKRA Colloqium on Testing and Assessment Proceedings
Editors, Denis Vincent, A. K. Pugh and Greg Brooks

In preparation:

Primary Care: Social and Personal Education in Primary Schools
Dr Kenneth David and Dr Tony Charlton

Assessing and Teaching Language: Literacy and Oracy in Schools
Mary Neville

Children Becoming Readers

Henry Pearson

MACMILLAN
EDUCATION

First published 1987
Reprinted 1989

Published by
MACMILLAN EDUCATION LTD
Houndmills, Basingstoke, Hampshire RG21 2XS
and London
Companies and representatives
throughout the world

Printed in Hong Kong

British Library Cataloguing in Publication Data
Pearson, Henry
Children becoming readers.
1. Reading
I. Title
428.4'3   LB1050
ISBN 0-333-44589-9
ISBN 0-333-44590-2 Pbk

The author wishes to thank Gary Lloyd for the cartoons.

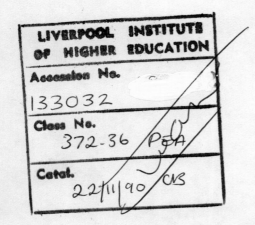

Contents

Practical Boxes

For Emma and Tessa

Introduction

While more and more subjects and disciplines come flooding into the
school curriculum, each demanding additional time, resources and
expertise, it is not surprising that teachers feel the pressure of having to
learn more and more information and new ways of organising and
presenting material. Yet, as a classroom teacher, I have always been
impressed by the confidence with which children cope with innovation
and take up the challenge to learn. Many books are written about ways
of teaching children to do mathematics, play music, operate computers,
develop literacy and all the varied activities they are presented with in
school. Fewer books, if any, have concerned themselves with teaching
children to learn. There is a simple reason for this – children don't need
to be taught to learn; they do it anyway! What is more, they do it with
ease and alacrity. Children learn an enormous amount during their early
years, and they continue to learn when they enter school. In fact, they
are learning every minute of the day and it is impossible to stop them.
However, the problem is that children don't always learn what we would
like them to learn, and they don't necessarily learn what we teach them.
Teachers and educationalists decide what is to be taught, whilst children
themselves decide what is to be learned. The challenge for schools, then,
is to draw the three strands together – the curriculum, the teaching and
the learning.

The learning which children successfully accomplish before they enter
school is considerable. Perhaps most impressive is the ease with which
children learn the conventions of speech. This has implications for
children learning to read, not so much because the two activities, talking
and reading, are similar, but rather because, by learning to talk, children
have already demonstrated that they are disposed to learn. What is
more, they have displayed a disposition to learn an activity which is
astonishingly complex. So, children have become proficient learners long
before they come to school. They learn to talk by listening to others

talking, by engaging in talk with others and by using talk themselves. This exemplifies a perfect partnership between learning and teaching, but only if the true origin of the verb 'to teach' is adopted – that is, 'to demonstrate'. In other words, children learn to talk by people demonstrating to them how it is done, through a partnership between learner and teacher.

In terms of reading, such a partnership can manifest itself in several ways. For example, children will benefit from seeing their teachers read, not only for the purpose of being shown how it is done, but also to demonstrate that reading is not something that teachers tell children to do without doing it themselves. Teachers should read with the children and help them with their reading rather than intimidating children by placing them in testing situations. Teachers can also demonstrate to children how reading style is varied according to purpose. Finally, the partnership needs to extend to involve parents, other adults, teachers and other children; the ideal classroom atmosphere is one in which children cooperate and help each other with their learning. Just as children develop their speech by talking with others, so reading can be developed by children reading with others.

Most importantly, reading needs to be viewed by children as a worthwhile, useful and enjoyable activity; this book endeavours to suggest how these three requirements might be satisfied in the classroom. Chapter 1 entitled 'Introducing Children to Reading' describes the early development of literacy and approaches for ensuring that reading is made easy, meaningful and enjoyable for children. Chapters 2 and 3 consider the application of reading abilities: 'Reading to Learn' describes some functional aspects of reading, whilst 'Reading to Create' looks at children's responses to fiction. Chapter 4 considers two issues related to literacy – reading problems and assessment. Finally some reviews of recent publications concerned with children's reading are included, under the heading 'Sources'.

Throughout the text, practical suggestions for classroom activities are presented in two ways. 'Practical Boxes' are placed strategically throughout the first three chapters and offer ideas for classroom work arising out of the theoretical discussion which surrounds them. In addition to these, Chapters 2 and 3 both end with sections describing case studies of topic approaches undertaken in one primary classroom.

Chapter 1

Introducing Children to Reading

Reading issues

'If you can read this, thank a teacher' sports a car rear window's sticker, designed presumably to promote the teacher image in the public eye. The assertion is bold, and this chapter considers whether the teachers are justified and what they might do to enhance their claim.

The sticker may have been pasted with some hesitation because, in spite of the many publications, courses and conferences on the subject of reading, or maybe because of them, there is still some uncertainty in schools about what the process of learning involves and how best to introduce children to the skill of reading. The result is that children are often confronted with reading programmes that are unconvincing, with methods that vary from teacher to teacher and with materials which bear little relationship to the reading process itself.

Perhaps most disturbing is the fact that reading has become too big an issue. From all quarters there is pressure on children to learn to read as early and as quickly as possible. It is hardly surprising, therefore, that many develop a resistance to reading and anything associated with it. The effect of such pressure is manifested not only in children who fail to learn to read but also in those who do learn but cease to become readers thereafter. *cf The strugglers   Tony Martin*

Present evidence would seem to suggest that many of our reading programmes are less than effective. Both primary and secondary special needs departments are flourishing, the dyslexia movement has become a growth industry by having deceptively made illiteracy respectable and many adults succeed in emerging illiterate from eleven years' formal education. *Tony Martin*

Fortunately though, the sticker designer can gain reassurance and support from the many children who do enjoy reading and who become habitual book users. Of course, one cannot expect all children to engage

so fully in the reading experience, in rather the same way that we have no right to expect all children to become keen musicians. Nevertheless, schools do have an obligation to introduce children to music and books in as appetising a way as possible. In this way, decisions that children make regarding acceptance or rejection are based on a reasonable understanding and appreciation of what each of the activities involves. I suggest that it is particularly important for teachers to do justice to reading since books provide access to a range of thoughts, feelings, emotions, ideas, adventure, excitement and information which no one person could experience first hand and which few other media can rival.

Reading approaches

Although it is acknowledged here that approaches used to introduce children to reading, and reading to children, will depend to some extent on teacher style, child idiosyncracy and environmental constraints, I maintain that any approach should have three essential ingredients: it should be *easy*, *meaningful* and *enjoyable*. It is likely that the last will obtain if the first two apply – that is, reading will be enjoyable if it is made easy and meaningful.

Making reading easy

Many approaches used in schools make learning to read difficult. Such approaches deny children much of the information they need to work out and understand what reading is all about. In order to appreciate this point it is helpful to understand that reading is a system involving various features and components working together and in conjunction with each other. A reader can operate successfully only if aware of the whole system and the way that it works. A comparison can be drawn here between reading and talking. Talking is also a system involving the simultaneous interaction of sound, structure and meaning. Almost all children learn to understand speech and to use the system of talking easily and with no formal instruction. By being exposed to speech, by listening to fluent talkers using the whole system and by being immersed in opportunities to use the system themselves in meaningful and purposeful situations, children become talkers – and how!

Because young children are particularly adept at working out systems, and because the language skills of talking and reading have much in common, it follows that the sorts of techniques used to introduce children to oral language can be used also with reading. In other words, reading can be made similarly easy.

It would be inappropriate and ineffective, for example, to attempt to teach children to talk by first breaking the skill down into its component parts. Imagine trying to teach sounds in order that children could eventually build up words; imagine introducing words to be eventually arranged into sentences. In fact, imagine trying to 'teach' children to talk at all.

Hall (1985) highlights the natural language process through which children can learn to listen, talk, read and write:

> Just as children would not learn to talk if deprived of access to language and appropriate social experiences with language, so children will not learn literacy unless they see print and experience print being used in appropriate ways. (p. 58)

Yet many of the reading methods used in schools are inappropriate. In the mistaken belief that children can cope with only a small amount of information at a time, reading is often broken down into its component sub-skills which are then taught one by one. Children are required to master each of these skills before endeavouring to piece the jigsaw together to make sense of the whole reading picture.

Teachers often claim a high percentage of success in the use of such strategies claiming that children in their care have become proficient at the sub-skills of, for example, letter sound correspondence or word recognition. However, in so doing, they are describing a hazardous and circuitous route which is unlikely to be efficacious in producing complete, efficient and committed readers. This is because such piecemeal strategies have lost sight of the fact that it is ideas that readers read, not words and sounds. It is sentences that give words meaning and not the other way round. If children are to make sense of their reading, if reading is to be made easy for them, it is the meaning, the system and the ideas that they need to be introduced to, rather than the surface features of the text.

In spite of this, some recent publications on the subject perpetuate the piecemeal approach. *Reading: Teaching for Learning* by Vera Southgate (1984) suggests that children should be introduced to reading by being given lists and collections of words to learn. 'If a child is to be able to read continuous prose with understanding' says Southgate, 'the first prerequisite is that he needs to recognise instantly, on sight, approximately 99 per cent of the words in the text' (p. 12). Her programme of word games, boxes of words to take home and learn, flash cards and a Friday revision session is recommended to last for 'a year or two, or maybe longer with slow learning children or remedial groups' (p. 38). Could it be that it is strategies such as this that actually produce slow learners and remedial groups?

At one point, Southgate cites the use of the tachistoscope – a device used in the Second World War to flash up images of aeroplane silhouettes to assist pilots in the instant recognition of enemy aircraft. This is the precursor of the popular flash cards which, based on the same principle as the tachistoscope, are supposed to assist children in the instant recognition of words. However, the problem with this comparison is that aeroplanes, unlike words, do not arrange themselves into meaningful sentences. The very advantage that language offers is lost once words are treated in isolation as is inevitable with the flash card approach. These cards, and other whole word/look and say devices, deprive children of the wealth of information they could be using to work out and remember the words, and they do little to alert children to the system of reading. After the 'year or two, or even longer' that Southgate prescribes for these word-attack activities, the children must wonder what this thing called reading is all about! Ironically, later in her book, Southgate suggests that such activities and games should occupy only a small proportion of the children's time, and that the major portion should be devoted to 'learning to read by reading'. I wonder, therefore, why the whole-word

approaches, which occupy so large a portion of Southgate's book, are necessary in the first place.

Any approach that isolates one aspect of reading is likely to be confusing for children. Similar objections can be levelled at over reliance on phonic approaches which introduce reading by breaking down words into their component sounds. By being able to recognise the sound that each letter, or group of letters, makes, the child is required to build up the word. This is especially difficult given that the sound symbol relationship of the English language is so notoriously inconsistent. Take, for example, the sound of the letter 'o' in *women*, *hot*, *monkey* and *donkey*, or the 'a' sound in *any*, *half*, *hand* and *all*. Over 40% of the words in this paragraph suffer from the same inconsistency, including such key words as 'any', 'one', 'to', 'so' and 'the'.

I am not necessarily suggesting that readers need not be equipped with phonic and word-attack skills, though I am challenging the way that these skills are often taught. After all, as mature readers we use both in our reading. If, for example, you are unfamiliar with the word 'adumbrated', you might resort to phonic strategies in order to help you decipher the word. However, that you can say the word 'adumbrated' does not mean that you can read it, especially if the word is not in your mental lexicon and particularly if you are provided with no other clues to help you to understand the word. On the other hand, if the word had been presented to you in context – for example, 'Owing to lack of time the chairperson simply adumbrated the programme to be followed the next day' – then you would be in a better position to speculate that the word means something like 'outlined' and thus to read and remember it. In other words, the more clues that children can be given and the more strategies they are able simultaneously to bring to bear in deciphering words, the easier the task. 'Reading' says Smith (1984), 'makes you good at phonics, rather than phonics making you good at reading' (p. 11).

> ### Introducing reading components
>
> A better way of alerting children to the components of reading is to draw their attention to phonic and whole-word devices during the process of natural and meaningful reading. For example, you might read a story to them so that they can follow the text with you. On subsequent readings, the children can join in with you when they feel able. Having done this a few times start to highlight features of the text, for example, picking out words that share the same initial letter sound, or finding all instances of the use of the word 'when' or 'big' or 'beautiful'. Different coloured print can be used to draw attention to these so that the children are learning their phonic and word-attack skills, but in the context of meaningful reading.

Any approach that relies heavily on either phonic or whole-word methods is likely to be inadequate. Yet Beech (1985) in his book *Learning to Read* seems unaware of alternatives. In summarising his chapter on teaching children to learn to read, he recommends that 'the first stages of reading can normally be approached in two different ways – namely the whole word and phonic approaches'. He goes on to say that 'children can be taught by either method, but inevitably the alternative approach has to be used at some stage'. Beech then argues that 'the first stage involving the acquisition of basic reading skills has to be mastered to a certain level in order that resources can be made available for understanding fully what reading is all about' (p. 41). It is no wonder that Waterland (1985) writes of 'children who have been taught to read but have failed to learn it' (p. 11).

Making reading meaningful

Whole-word and phonic approaches are based on misinterpreted theories of perception – that is, that in reading the eye sees the information and passes it to the brain to be processed. However, this is clearly not the case. As a result of research into the relationship between thought and language, psycholinguists maintain that, in the process of reading, the brain tells the eye as much as the eye tells the brain.

If perception were paramount, we should be able to read any print provided that we could see it and distinguish the shapes. Of course this is not the case, for if the print uses a system of symbols with which we are unfamiliar, then no amount of perception will enable us to read it. Already we have an instance of the brain supplying insufficient information to enable us to read, in this case, information about the lettering.

But what if we see a lettering system which is familiar?

> Juma anataka kupiga mpira.
> Ali amepiga mpira juu.

If you do not know the Swahili language then you will have difficulty reading this, so your brain is supplying insufficient help, in this case, about the language system. Incidentally, you could probably sound the message out since Swahili is written as spoken, but you would still be unable to understand it. In which case one can say that reading is taking place only when the message is being received and understood. Much that we accost children with in school must seem like Swahili to them!

So, now we'll look at a lettering system and a language that you can understand:

> While people construct a sense of identity by a synthesis of early childhood identifications with a large number of later commitments and loyalties, occupational identity has probably become a much more significant component of total identity in modern society than in the past. In an industrial society, it is primarily occupational status which is ranked in superior and inferior grades by the spontaneous process of stratification. (Blauner, p. 30)

In this case the language is appropriate and probably most of the words are familiar, but what does it mean? Unless you are conversant with sociological jargon you will have difficulty in understanding the message.

Unfortunately, many devices and materials presented to children in the guise of reading are in fact meaningless. What is the meaning of 'is' or 'in' or 'and' or 'a' or 'the'? Since all learning depends upon the efficient storage and retrieval of information then meaning is essential if learners of reading are to build up a store of readily recognisable words. The old tin containing word cards to be remembered will be as easily forgotten unless they are presented in a context which gives them meaning. It is meanings that we remember, that we are able to incorporate into the organised system of the brain, not arbitrary symbols. The words of a poem are easier to remember than the same number of random digits.

But let us now reverse the situation in our examples of the importance of the brain in informing the eye whilst reading. Can you complete this sentence?

> Jane could never remember to do anything. She had even ****** to buy the bread that her mother had asked her to get.

You probably had little trouble in recognising the word as *forgotten*, yet interestingly you could not see the word at all. On this occasion your brain advised your eye and supplied the information.

Here is another example:

> John's father taught him to nid. He practised it often and was an accomplished ****** by the time he got to school.

In this peculiar example, your brain supplied your eye with a word which you had neither seen nor heard before and which doesn't even exist (except in this book). And I maintain that your eye has been informed because you can even spell the word as well – *nidder*!

We can now use this same principle to illustrate how the brain appears to function for a child at the early stage of learning to read. The missing word below represents one which the reader may not have seen before – or at least, does not remember.

> When school finished, Robert rushed home as ****** as he could to see if Felix was still there.

Taking into account the meaning of the sentence and the clues from the surrounding words, one can hazard a guess that the word is either *rapidly*, *fast*, *quickly* or *soon*. The first question to ask is 'Does getting the exact word matter?' Any one of these words is contextually viable and enables the reader to continue and enjoy the story. However, one needs only to be supplied with the initial letter 'q . . .' to know that the word must be *quickly*. And in terms of learning to read, children are more likely to remember the word on future occasions because it was introduced in a meaningful context and because, on the first visual encounter, they worked it out for themselves.

A further point to note from this example is that rather than phonic knowledge being relied upon to decipher the word, response to the initial letter sound enabled the reader to *confirm* the word. This is especially important since the word *quickly* was most likely to have been in the child's arsenal of spoken words. After all, there would have been little point in 'sounding out' a word that the reader probably knew already but had simply not seen before.

Reading systems

At this point it would be useful to examine more closely the system of reading which was described above as 'various features and components working together and in conjunction with each other'. Reading involves response to a system of cues which help us to decipher words and meanings, both familiar and unfamiliar. The four components of this system are *structural*, *semantic*, *bibliographic* and *graphophonic* cues.

Structural cues

Structural cues in the text interact with our knowledge of the grammar (the form of words) and the syntax (the order of words) of the language.

This knowledge is drawn from our ability to talk and from our experience with written language. (It was this cue system that enabled you to decipher *nidder* in the John extract above.)

Semantic cues

Semantic cues derived from the meaning of the text interact with our knowledge of the world and things in it drawn from life's experiences, including reading. (It was this cue system that enabled you to decipher *forgotten* in the Jane extract above.)

Bibliographic cues

Bibliographic cues are derived from the organisation and presentation of the text – the illustrations, layout, headings, captions, tables, graphs and so on. These are of particular help to children during the early stages of learning to read.

Graphophonic cues

Graphophonic cues are supplied by the spelling and presentation of the words which interact with our knowledge of word recognition and phonic analysis. (It was this cue system that enabled you to confirm the word *quickly* in the Robert extract above.)

These four cues systems act simultaneously and in conjunction with each other. By using the four sets of cues one is responding to the whole system of reading – structure, meaning, organisation and presentation. A full use of all four systems makes for more efficient reading; recourse to only one does not.

A useful analogy can be drawn here between the systems of reading and a car with its four wheels. For safe and efficient driving, one needs all four wheels to travel on. However, a car recently advertised on television demonstrated that it is possible to remove one wheel and travel fairly safely on three. Some stunt artists are even able to drive on two! But such people are already efficient and experienced drivers; this is not a strategy to be taught at driving school. You will notice that nobody has yet succeeded in driving on one wheel – not when there are four available.

Early fluent readers

All too often the teaching profession adopts the attitude that it is the custodian of some secret formula for teaching reading and that the work must start from scratch when the children enter school. This inevitably ignores the major influence of preschool experience in the environment outside the classroom and at home.

Up to this point, children have started to learn about reading in a natural, often incidental way. Smith (1984) describes children's induction to what he calls the 'literacy club' and suggests that children learn 'usually without anyone being aware that they are learning – by participating in literate activities with people who know how and why to do these things' (p. 7). There is evidence to suggest that children are already paid up members of the literacy club before they enter school.

Indeed, it is unlikely that children could avoid some form of exposure to the printed word in their environment. Bills through the letter box, labels in supermarkets, advertisements on television, newspapers, road signs, food packets and shopping lists all contribute to a veritable Niagara of words.

I conducted a small experiment with a group of five-year olds who had just started school; the idea was to find out how many of these environmental words they could recognise. Amongst the words selected for use were *Asda*, *Cornflakes*, *The 'A' Team*, *Ariel*, *The Sun* and *Toyota*. When these were presented to them in handwritten form, a few of the twelve children recognised one or two of the words. When presented using the familiar lettering style associated with these words, success in recognition was about 50%. However, when the words were presented in the context in which they are popularly seen – for example, a photograph of the Asda building with sign board, a packet of cornflakes and a video of the Ariel television advertisement (without soundtrack), then most of the children recognised most of the words.

It was apparent that the children were aware of the existence of these words and the meaning they represent. When presented with a photograph of a road sign, one child said 'That tells my mummy which way to go'! The fact that they were helped by the visual presentation of the word suggests that they were using a form of bibliographic cue and, like words in a surrounding text, were better able to decipher words when they were presented in the context in which they usually appear.

In a society in which words surround us it is reasonable to assume that most children have some sort of awareness of print, although this is not to say that all children have enjoyed a similar quality of experience in their preschool lives. One of our responsibilities as teachers, then, is to extend the experiences of children whose introduction has been rich and varied, and to compensate for those whose experiences have been largely incidental. Amongst those entering the infant school reception class there may well be some who can already read. For these children it is highly inappropriate to subject them to a programme of prereading activities or even formal introductions to phonics and whole word recognition. Rather, we need to build on such children's existing knowledge in extending their reading in meaningful situations. I suggest that this same principle applies to all children, regardless of experience and ability.

Much research into reading problems has concentrated on those children who are having difficulty with their reading. The results are then accompanied by recommendations for remedial action focusing on specific aspects of the reading task which are presenting difficulties – for example, phonic analysis, word memory, response to context cues and so on. The problem with this approach is that the more specific the treatment, the further from real reading these programmes become. The clinical situations in which such programmes are invariably conducted do little to assist children in travelling on the four reading wheels.

Less research has taken the more common sense view of scrutinising what it is about the quality of experiences that early *fluent* readers have enjoyed which has facilitated their precocity. An understanding of the strategies by which such children have acquired an appetite for reading might help in designing compensatory work in schools for other children.

In her study of young fluent readers at the age of five, Clark (1976 and 1984) found that success in reading was not associated with any conscious attempt by parents to teach their children to read, nor was it connected with social class or size of family. These children were provided with plenty of opportunities for reading and many of the children had access to books in public libraries. Most of the children appear to have read silently either from the beginning or at an early age.

Ingham's study (1982) into the contrasting backgrounds of avid readers on the one hand and infrequent readers at the age of ten to twelve years on the other, concluded that 'none of the infrequent readers had stories read or told to them when they were small. . . . All the avid readers had stories read and/or told to them regularly by parents or grandparents' (p. 170).

The importance of the home influence on young fluent readers' success, combined with the fact that children's preschool experiences seem to do much to make them aware of the nature of reading, highlights the importance of providing continuity between school and preschool approaches to reading. Unfortunately, many of the approaches that children are subjected to at school are in sharp contrast to the sorts of experiences that many children enjoy at home.

From homes which present reading as a pleasurable activity, children in school come up against programmes in which pleasure is replaced by pressure – that is, pressure to work and learn to read with the promise of pleasure and enjoyment later. At home the children may have access to a variety of books with rich and often quite advanced language. In school some early reading programmes use no books at all, or perhaps, for each child, one book at a time with such threadbare language as:

> My house has a roof.
> It is a red roof.
> The roof of my house is red.

The pleasure and nourishment that children derive from listening to favourite stories read several times is replaced in school by the attitude that to return is regression and that we must get on to the next book in the scheme. This is hardly surprising though, in view of the fact that so many books used in school are not worth returning to.

From being read to at home, in school the child is suddenly given responsibility for most of the reading and, as a result, may see little of what the experienced reader does. Opportunities to read independently and possibly silently are at a premium in school where so much of the reading that children do is aloud and to the teacher.

To summarise, the three main conditions which appear to have contributed to early fluent reading are:

1. The children had access to a range of appetising books.
2. The children read independently, and often silently, either initially or from an early age and were encouraged to choose freely from the books available.
3. The children had been read to.

We can now take these three conditions and consider how they might be harnessed to benefit work in the classroom.

Reading materials

Up to this point we have concentrated on how children learn to read and the processes involved. But no process can be developed successfully without something of substance to read, without materials that will engage the reader and without books that are worth reading.

And yet it has been known for teachers to introduce children to reading using no books at all. Many prereading programmes have this effect; children are given exercises in left to right orientation, visual discrimination and sequencing using materials that are not related to books in any way. This must be rather like trying to learn to swim without water. Even amongst those books which are used as part of the resources for early reading programmes, there are some that are so dry and uninteresting that they must actually put children off reading – rather like learning to swim in mud. Amongst these muddy books I would place many that feature in reading schemes. These are books where the story is either of little value or, in some cases, non-existent. This is because the story has been sacrificed in the name of structure; books in which the authors have become so preoccupied with their own thoughts on what the process of reading might involve that the content, the very thing which should give a book its reason for existence, has been forgotten. Thus children are exposed to texts in which key words are repeated ad nauseam, in which attempts have been made to produce phonically consistent texts resulting in ludicrously stilted prose and in which simplicity has been confused with paucity. Such books are unlikely to interest children; without interest we deny them of their most important incentive for learning.

One of the problems is that, as educators, we can become so absorbed by the process of learning and the need for constant progress that we forget the learners themselves and what they need. The children's interest and concern is with the content. They will develop a positive attitude to reading only if what they read appeals to them. Chronologically, a disposition to learn comes before the acquisition of skill.

In their excellent book *On Learning to Read*, Bettelheim and Zelan (1982) have this to say about our focus in teaching reading:

> If, rather than concentrating on developing reading skills educational efforts from the very beginning were concentrated on the desire to become literate – essentially an inner attitude to reading – then the final result might be that a much larger segment of the population would be literate. (p. 21)

My own feeling is that many children are put off reading at the crucial early stage because of the poor quality of materials that they are expected to read. Proponents of the use of reading schemes, for example, suggest that it is the structure which such books can offer that is so valuable. Thus teachers who would normally subscribe to a child-centred approach to learning are to be seen using materials that represent the antithesis to their own belief. In defending their use of schemes, teachers claim that they offer a structure which few have either the time or the ability to provide. However, I would question whether it is appropriate to even attempt to structure reading at all. In common with

of the strugglers
(transcript)

talking it is not an activity that lends itself to a stage by stage approach. Besides which, to prescribe a structure that is to suit all children is to ignore the individual learning styles and strategies that each child displays.

The D.I.Y. Book

This gives children the opportunity to create their own book whilst having much of the spade work done for them. A story book is prepared by the teacher with pictures on one side of the page and simple text on the other. However the pictures and text are removed leaving a blank book. The idea is that the children reassemble the book creating the story in what they think is the right sequence and matching picture with text. The effect is best achieved by using velcro to attach the pieces to the book. In this way, one blank book could be used to house several stories.

In an attempt to accommodate this individualised aspect to children's learning, many schools have adopted an eclectic approach by incorporating several schemes simultaneously into their reading programmes. This is presumably in the hope that somewhere amongst all these different structures each child will be able to find one which is appropriate. Bernice and Cliff Moon (1986) describe the use of their 'individualised reading programme' which enables children to draw from a variety of schemes and other books at a level appropriate to their needs. The Moons offer some valuable criteria for the selection of books to be included in their collection. These criteria include a consideration of whether each book is worth reading, is designed to 'ease' reading or is culturally biased. The reading level of each book is then assessed, not by the use of tests and indices but according to the ability of children to read them. As they say: 'The concepts of readability on which these lists are based depends upon the interaction between the reader and the text' (p. 5).

In principle this all appears most satisfactory. From this now wider range each child is more likely to find good books that will appeal. Unfortunately, this advantage is then lost the moment the books are grouped together and coded into stages according to readability. This is because some teachers limit children to books within a particular colour

range, however wide and varied this may be, and preclude them from enjoying books that they may find appetising but that are not within their prescribed colour. Amongst such books may be those old favourites which children are naturally inclined to return to and reread, and also those ostensibly difficult books which children, driven by interest or curiosity, might like to have a go at.

Perhaps of most concern is the competitive element which is almost bound to accrue when children are designated to particular stages. Though we may attempt to disguise the fact by using colours instead of numbers, children are well aware of differences and become conscious of the fact that some are on a 'higher' colour than others. Of course, many children excel in the face of competition, but is this the most desirable motive for reading? A more valuable motive is derived from an intrinsic interest in the activity itself rather than a desire to 'do better than thy neighbour'. Besides which, competition is likely to be counterproductive, even disturbing, for those that invariably find themselves on 'lower' colours.

Coding books

An interesting adaptation of the individualised reading system is proposed by Prentice (1985) who suggests coding books that have first of all satisfied the requirement of a 'real' book into the following 6 levels:

Whites: no text;

Reds: simple repetitive text with strong picture cues;

Yellows: simple text with strong picture and semantic cues;

Greens: more involved text which does not rely totally on above cues; children need to use other forms of decoding, including initial letter phonic cues.

Blues: children have a fairly wide reading vocabulary, including most of the common prepositions and other non-noun words and use a variety of cues in decoding unknown words.

Browns: children are reading fluently, with little or no difficulty. (p. 72)

This seems to be a very useful classification system. Prentice then goes on to explain that 'Each child would be allocated to the appropriate colour for his level of reading for formal reading sessions, but would make use of all colours as he desired when reading informally' (p. 72). I feel that this rather spoils the practice for I wonder why reading needs to be divided into formal and informal. Nevertheless, given that all reading can be treated according to Prentice's informal approach, with children making use of all colours, then the system is a most useful one. Would it not be possible, for example, to explain to the children what the colour coding represents so that they can be aware of what to expect from the book when choosing it? Alternatively, it could serve as a guide to the teacher in counselling children about which book they might want to read next.

My intention is not to dismiss reading scheme books out of hand. Some of them are excellent and worth reading; they are often selected by children when given a free choice. I am only questioning the desirability of using them in any structured way.

The ultimate test of a real book is whether or not children like to read it. However, Waterland (1985) suggests that a useful test is to see if it reads aloud well, is entertaining and sounds right. She suggests that 'if the teacher cannot stand the book, it will be impossible to share it successfully with the child' (p. 36). Somerfield (1983) recommends that books should be relevant and asks 'Do children recognise in the book any aspects of their own everyday life, or their inner world of imagination and fantasy' (p. 24)?

In advising parents about the number of books that should be available for children to choose from, Meek (1982) recommends that there should be 'as many as you would expect your child to have if they were toys' (p. 95). However, even several hundred books of the most admirable quality are of little use unless they are available in the classroom and displayed in a way that makes them accessible and appetising. Centrally situated school libraries are less than useful if a pilgrimage is required for the child to fetch a book, or worse still, if the only time for changing books is during a once weekly class library lesson.

Having established some principles concerning the selection and deployment of books, we can now consider what use might be made of them.

Reading independence

This section begins with the story of Stephen and Christopher. At the age of eight, neither of them had learnt to read. It was the beginning of the school year of my first teaching post and I was anxious to do all the right things; this included launching these two into their reading careers. During the busy working day I seemed unable to find time to give them the special attention I thought they needed and because of this I decided to devote fifteen minutes of each lunchtime to helping them. In order that I could attend to their individual needs, I decided to work with Christopher for the first two weeks and after that transfer my attention to Stephen. However, Stephen was still anxious to attend the sessions, so I suggested that he might like to make use of his time by looking at the books which had just been housed in our newly established book corner. Meanwhile I administered to Christopher a concentrated programme of phonic games and whole word activities. By the end of a fortnight he had become quite good at some of the games but, to my great disappointment, he had still not learnt to read. Somewhat disillusioned I turned my attention to Stephen. I need not have bothered; he had taught himself to read!

Both of these children had a history of failure in their reading and neither had succeeded in mastering the so-called 'basic skills' from the programmes they had been given. As Stephen explained, he had always been promised that he would be able to read books once he could read. It had not occurred to anyone, including me at that time, that the best way of learning to read was by reading, and reading means using books. Stephen's parents were delighted; they gave me chocolates. But the reward was undeserved – it was Stephen and the books that had done it, not I.

I am not suggesting that all children will learn to read in the way that Stephen did. I am suggesting that many children will absorb reading without any formal instruction *if given the opportunity to do so*. Should this be possible it must surely be the most satisfactory and painless way of learning, but it will only happen if provision is made for all children to have access to good books and time to read them.

Time for independent reading might enable some children to become readers. For those that don't learn in this way the experience is nevertheless invaluable. By browsing through and handling books, the children can savour the pictures, practise turning over the pages, familiarise themselves with the sequencing and learn how books work. What more appropriate prereading activity than this?

Furthermore, this provides one of the few classroom activities that is suited to children at all stages of development. The readers have a chance to practise, the non-readers have a chance to learn, and all have the essential opportunity to enjoy books.

Finding the time and the place

In order for independent reading sessions to work, provision needs to be made to display all the books to their best advantage, with as many 'full frontal' as possible. There also needs to be a space for children to both wander round the books and to sit, lounge, relax and enjoy them. But both these requirements are academic unless children are allowed time to indulge in such reading. All too often children are allowed to look at the books only when they have finished their work, in which case some children never get the chance because they seldom finish work, and these are probably the ones that most need it. Some schools set aside a time for silent reading in which everyone, including the teacher, the head and, in one case I heard of, the caretaker as well, sit quietly and read their books. Another possibility is to weave silent reading sessions into the fabric of the day. Whichever approach is used, children need to appreciate that reading is an activity which is regarded highly by the teacher and the school, not as important work but as a valuable time of enjoyment. Independent reading needs to be promoted to the First Division and not relegated to the Southern League.

So far I have been describing situations in which children can be encouraged to read silently and independently. In reality what many children do is to read the books aloud to themselves. Or rather, the children tell the story in their own words, often taking great liberties with the author's text. Based on the illustrations, or perhaps as a result of having had the story read to them, the children fabricate their own narrative. They 'read' the story with expression and zest, turning over the pages at the appropriate time, completely absorbed in the book. The result, as anyone who has experienced this phenomenon knows, is delightful. The point is that where it happens it should be applauded and encouraged, for the children who engage in what Holdaway (1979) calls 'reading-like behaviour', have actually learnt almost all that there is to know about reading. Reading-like behaviour is closer to real reading than most of the contrived pre and early-reading activities that many children are required to do in the guise of reading.

We are talking here about experiences that should be encouraged rather than about skills which should be taught. Thus we provide reading experiences which will enable the already initiated readers to extend, and the novices to develop their abilities. For all children such opportunities will help to foster the essential 'inner attitude' to the task of reading which should precede the skill. The final section of this chapter examines an activity that occupies so much of the infant teacher's time and attention – listening to children read.

Reading aloud

It has already been suggested that many children, like the avid readers in Ingham's study, had read silently and had been read to from an early age. In schools, much of the reading that children do is aloud and to the teacher. Indeed, many teachers expend a great deal of time and effort in listening to children read. This invariably poses enormous problems in attempting to give sufficient attention to all children and to all areas of the curriculum simply because the exercise of hearing each child read frequently is so time consuming. I met one teacher who had overcome such administrative difficulties by hearing children read two at a time from different texts! I use the word 'hear' advisedly, for this teacher would surely have been unable to *listen* to both.

It seems to be a common belief that children are learning to read only when reading aloud and that any other reading activity is supplementary. In fact I am suggesting something quite different: that more favourable conditions for learning occur when children are being read to.

Reading to children can be efficacious in several ways, especially when children are able to follow the text and see what the reader is doing with it. Here the novice readers are put into a genuine learning situation, apprenticed, as they are, to the accomplished reader in action. In such a reading situation, the novices witness the whole system of reading in use, in much the same way that they have already learnt to use the system of talking.

In considering the initial phase of learning to read and write, Teale (1984) proposes four aspects necessary for the development of literacy skills. These are an understanding of the functions and uses of written language, a grasp of the concepts of print – how books work, what reading is and the form and structure of written language, an attitude towards reading and a knowledge of reading strategies. Teale maintains that reading aloud to children is beneficial in developing these aspects and that being read to 'is one type of experience that delightfully and effectively ushers a child into the world of literacy' (p. 120).

Unfortunately, the value of reading to children as a device for teaching reading is often not recognised; many regard the activity as filigree to entertain children for the last fifteen minutes of the school day. Francis (1982) for example, in describing a reading programme for children in their first year at school, makes no mention of reading to children as an instructional device.

When children are being read to the pressure is taken off, leaving them free to concentrate on the business of learning. The climate created for children when having to read aloud may be so overwhelming and demanding that one can hardly expect them to learn from it. Very few people actually learn in the process of being tested. The business of having to sound out all the words precisely and accurately occupies so much of the children's attention that they are distracted from the elements of the text which will most assist them in learning to read – that is, the substance of the ideas in the story and the way that the words and sentences combine to create meaning.

When following a text which someone else is reading aloud, the novice is able to bring structural, semantic, bibliographic and graphophonic cues simultaneously to bear in making predictions about what will come next. These predictions are then confirmed, rejected or refined in the light of the text being heard. In this way the children are not just passively sounding out the words but are instead given responsibility for their own learning. In much the same way that a scientist

learns from experiments, so the young reader learns through hypothesis formulation and testing.

The essence of this 'shared reading' approach as an instructional device is in reading the stories several times with the children. On each occasion the experienced reader points to the words being read. The children soon become familiar with the story and the words used and are gradually able to join in with the read, either silently or aloud. As the pointing continues the children associate the words they are saying with those in the text, so that they are able to absorb the words in context. Since young children seem to have a remarkable ability to memorise, the approach is particularly effective. Many teachers will be familiar with occasions when they have sent a book home with a child who returns the next day and gaily recites the words having learnt the text off by heart. The temptation is to dismiss this as simply a ploy which does not really count as reading. The shared approach being recommended here, however, actually capitalises on the child's ability to remember; learning a text off by heart is seen as an asset, not an impediment, to reading. During their times for independent reading the children can take copies of books which have been read with them in this way, and practise reading them alone.

Using big books

Many publishers now produce big versions of their normal-sized reading books. These are extremely valuable for, as well as the novelty to the children of a big book, it enables the teacher to engage in shared reading experience with groups of children, or even the whole class. The big book experience simulates the intimacy of a one-to-one situation with a large group of children all of whom are able to see and read along with the text. These published big books are generally good, extremely useful but rather expensive. They can be augmented though with books made by the teacher or the children. These need not be elaborate; indeed, they may be rather hurriedly produced on sheets of newsprint so as to capitalise quickly on an idea that a group of children have just composed. Making the book oneself enables one to tailor the text to individual or group needs. For example, coloured text can be used to highlight particular words, or comon initial letters. In order to get the most potential out of big books, some normal-sized equivalents need to be available for children to read for themselves.

Reading is often, and understandably regarded by children as an insular and unsociable activity which is in conflict with the gregariousness which many young children display. The shared reading experience, on either a one-to-one or a group basis, is furnished with all the benefits of a cooperative and social occasion in which participants read together and engage in discussion about the story borne of a mutual enjoyment of the reading experience.

A language experience approach

This approach forges a connection for children between their talking and the reading experience. The activity described here is a development of this approach which focuses on the children re-arranging sentences to read. The activity is best done with a group of four children.
1. Before the session, mount a large sheet of paper (A3 size) onto a display board or easel. Using paper clips, attach four blank strips of paper to the top of the sheet.

2. Explain to the children that, as a group, they are going to create a picture. The children contribute descriptions of what the picture is to contain while the teacher draws what they are describing, at the same time questioning the children and encouraging them to expand and clarify their descriptions.
3. When the picture is completed each child contributes a sentence to describe the picture. The sentences are written by the teacher on the strips at the top of the sheet.
4. The children read through the sentences with the teacher as a shared reading experience.
5. Each strip is removed and with scissors is cut up into word units and given to the children to rearrange. Whilst the children are doing this, the teacher works with the children helping them to read the sentence and draws their attention to the individual words.
6. The children paste the sentence pieces together and return them to their original position above the picture. The picture with sentences is then available for use, rather like a big book, for reading on future occasions.

One objection levelled at approaches such as these is that they leave reading too much to chance; left to their own devices, it is suggested, children will only consolidate errors in their reading. On the other hand, many children will flourish in an unstructured environment; others may need more careful guidance. The main point is that any structuring is done by the teacher to suit the children rather than being imposed by some remote reading scheme creator. The job of the teacher, then, as well as to provide a rich and stimulating reading environment, is to monitor each child's progress and make appropriate reading materials available. Progress can be monitored by observing the children when reading, by talking with them about what they have read and the way they have tackled their reading, and by listening to the children read.

Children's reading aloud is being recommended here as an important, but supplementary part of the reading programme, and as one of a series of methods which can be used to monitor children's progress. In order for the method to be effective the children need more than just a couple of minutes out at the teacher's desk. Instead, they require the teacher's undivided attention for some five to ten minutes allowing time for discussion and careful scrutiny of the child's reading. Perhaps a better alternative to the formal, often rather public, teacher desk situation, is to create reading aloud opportunities from activities which children are engaged in and to conduct reading conferences where the children are working. The usefulness of reading conferences is discussed more fully in Chapter 4.

Paired reading

In any form, children's reading aloud is invariably monotonous, often meaningless and frequently unpopular with children. Perhaps a better bet for children is the paired reading approach described by Topping (1984). Here the adult and the child cooperate in the reading. The adult reads aloud and the child joins in if she wants to. Alternatively, the child takes the initiative and reads aloud calling upon the adult's help when required. The child signals the need for help with a prearranged nudge, then nudges again when she feels that she can continue unaided. Such reading experiences should happen in a relaxed atmosphere and should be a sharing, caring, discussing, reviewing and speculating book session – using of course, real books.

The approaches described in this chapter for introducing children to reading would hopefully constitute about a third of an infant-aged child's reading diet. At the same time children should be experiencing a whole range of other reading and allied activities: hearing, composing and acting out stories, talking, enjoying picture books, and using reading materials for more functional purposes. It is on these aspects of reading that attention is focused during the following chapters.

Chapter 2

Reading to Learn

Developing reading

In this chapter the focus changes from children learning to read to reading to learn. In particular the nature of reading comprehension is considered along with the way that reading style is adapted according to purpose, and some approaches to reading for information are examined. Finally, an example of a topic undertaken with a class of eight to nine year olds is described in order to illustrate how developing reading might be harnessed in the classroom.

However, although a distinction is made in this book between learning to read and reading to learn by assigning them to separate chapters, this is not to imply that the two should be separated in the curriculum. To begin with, if children are to understand what they are learning and if they are to appreciate the purposes of reading, they must experience reading being used in meaningful, purposeful and realistic ways, albeit at a rudimentary level, from the outset of their reading careers. Unless this happens, reading will be regarded by children as an abstract and academic activity – difficult to grasp and impossible to comprehend. Again, our analogy with talking applies here: it would be ludicrous to insist that children should learn the skill of talking first before being allowed to communicate and express themselves through speech.

A second reason for combining acquisition and use is to avoid perpetuating the idea that reading is initially to do with work with the promise of enjoyment later. If children are to develop a positive attitude to reading, the task must be viewed as enjoyable and satisfying from the start. As was suggested in Chapter 1 – children learn to read by reading.

Finally, all readers continue to develop their reading throughout their reading careers. Each time we read we are likely to perfect new strategies for approaching materials, all the time improving our reading. Nobody can ever really claim that they have fully learnt to read since we are

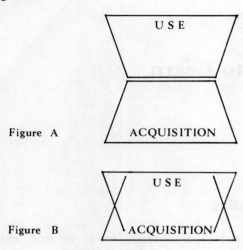

Figure A

Figure B

continually developing new abilities. So, learning to read and reading to learn are both ongoing and continual processes which should be intertwined in the way that we approach them in the classroom. This notion is well illustrated by Figures A and B based on an idea by Strang (1972). Figure B reflects the approach towards which we should be aiming.

For these reasons it is recommended that activities suggested in this chapter can be adapted and incorporated into early reading programmes to run alongside those suggested in Chapter 1. In fact, activities based on reading for information may be especially well suited to the needs of infants.

Traditionally, the majority of reading which children undertake, particularly in learning to read, is fiction. There are very good reasons for this, of course, not least of which is the fact that children enjoy a good story. However, from a technical point of view the reading of fiction makes particular demands. This is in the way that narrative requires a detailed and continuous read in order fully to follow the plot and to capture the flavour of the author's language – to hang, as it were, on every word. In contrast, to read specifically for information may be technically much less demanding: at its simplest level, the reader may be required merely to dip into the text in order to extract one word, sentence or fact. Children not yet able to read continuous prose can make good use of books as sources of information simply by locating and studying pictures. Here we have a good example of using reading at the initial stage of learning to read.

The treasure hunt

This is a suggestion for an approach to reading to learn which can be used even with reception children and certainly with second and third-year infants. The idea of the treasure hunt is to encourage children to locate, collect, organise and record information.

Imagine that a class of children is engaged in a topic on 'Animals'. How can the topic be developed to incorporate reading?

1. The teacher decides on eight animals to be investigated in this part of the topic. These might be: dog, cat, elephant, lion, horse, cow, giraffe and fish.

2. Find about four pictures of each. In fact, the main factor determining the choice of animal is the number of pictures that are available suitable for cutting out and posting on the wall. For each animal compose about half a dozen sentences each containing the name of the animal and describing it in some way. The sentences for the elephant might read something like:

> The elephant has a long trunk,
> The elephant's trunk helps him to feed,
> The skin of the elephant is grey,
> The elephant can reach up high with his trunk,
> Elephants live together in families.
> Some elephants have very large ears.

Each of these sentences is written on a separate strip of paper using quite large lettering.

3. Before the children come into the classroom fix the pictures and sentences around the classroom walls in no particular order — the more jumbled up the better.

4. When the children come into the classroom organise them into pairs. Each pair is given a card with the name of an animal written on it. In their pairs the children hunt for pictures of their animal and sentences that describe it. However, at this stage they are to leave the pictures and sentences where they are.

5. Arrange the children into groups of four, two pairs in each group. One pair now takes the other pair on a guided tour of their animal, showing them the pictures and reading them the sentences. The pairs then swap, and the other pair is shown around.

6. Back in the original pairs, the two children now go round and physically collect all the information about their animal.
7. Still working in pairs, the children now arrange the sentences and pictures into an order which they think is appropriate, matching sentence to picture as desired. Finally the strips and pictures are stuck, either into a specially prepared blank book or onto a large sheet of paper ready for display. Either way, the newly created resource is suitable for consumption and use by the rest of the class.

The teacher's role during all of this is to help the children with the task, particularly the reading of the sentences. Mind you, I have noticed in undertaking work like this that children display remarkable ability and initiative in reading the sentences for themselves, presumably because they are motivated through interest.

Implied in the distinction between the reading of narrative and reading for information is, what is in some ways, a false distinction between fiction and non-fiction. Many books written essentially for information purposes are presented in narrative form – for example, Dinosaur Books by Althea and many history books and biographies. Similarly, there is an information element in most stories, novels and poems. Perhaps more important is to consider the uses to which children might put books and the way that they might be encouraged to read them. Lavender (1983) maintains that 'when [children] can connect what they know, the questions they ask and what they find in books . . . they begin to use books for their own purposes in such a way as to make a nonsense of the artificial categories in which children's books are so often placed' (p. 9). The same criticism can be levelled then at distinctions made between textbooks and non-textbooks, reading scheme and non-reading scheme books.

However, books housed in libraries are classified and arranged under separate categories and in order for children to be able to make effective use of libraries they do need to understand how these classifications work. The answer would seem to be to expose children to as many different types of books as possible so that, through experience of use, they can learn what these types have to offer and how they might be read. Ultimately, if children are to become critically aware, it is they who should decide what use each book has for them.

Adult models of reading

If the use to which children put reading is to be realistic and if they are to practise reading, as Britton (1970) prescribes in the way that a doctor practises medicine and not in the way that a juggler practises a new trick before he performs it – then a major consideration in determining the way that reading is presented in the classroom is to have in mind the ways that adults read. The D.E.S. report (1975) *A Language for Life*, as its name implies recommends an approach to reading which is appropriate to the needs of adult life. By basing activities in the classroom on the sorts of reading that adults undertake using the sorts of real life materials that adults read, then we are more likely to help children to appreciate the relevance of reading tasks. Certainly the materials used should not be limited only to books but should include such environmental resources as pamphlets, brochures, timetables, menus, recipes, advertisements, manuals and so on. Such resources, as well as being potentially interesting, are often free!

Activities using environmental resources

The following suggestions are all designed, not just to use environmental resources but also to simulate real-life reading situations.

The railway booking office
1: A corner of the classroom is used to simulate a station booking office. This is then decorated with posters, racks containing brochures, timetables and maps. These could be the real articles acquired from the local railway station along with some designed and produced by the children.
2. The children act out, in pairs, situations in which one partner plays the part of the booking office clerk and the other a customer. The clerk can advise on the times of travel, route to be taken and the cost, eventually providing the customer with the appropriate ticket.

Cars for sale
This activity started when one of my class brought in a toy garage that his father had made him for Christmas. Three children decided to become second-hand car dealers. They studied the vehicles in the staff car park and noted down the details of each. These included the make and model, the registration number and

```
FIAT 128 SALOON. Taxed
and M.O.T. 47,000 miles
Good condition. Blue.
£700 o.n.o.
```

```
MINI 850. Red. L Reg.
62,000 miles. Radio.
Good condition. £350
```

```
FORD CORTINA. W Reg
1.6L White. No rust.
M.O.T. 30,000 miles.
£1800
```

year of manufacture, the current mileage and the colour. On returning to the classroom they referred to a recent motor magazine in order to find the list price of the cars. They then studied the local paper to learn how advertisements are phrased, and composed their own for the staff cars. Finally, they set out the garage with model cars representing those for sale and entertained customers with very elaborate explanations of the merits of their stock.

The Good Food Guide

I went round to all the cafés and restaurants in town asking for copies of menus. Back in the classroom the children set to work on writing a good food guide. This guide was to be arranged in sections. One group undertook research for their 'Fish-eaters guide' noting down the range, variety, quality and price of such meals in the various eating places. Other groups gave a similar treatment to meat, pancakes, hamburgers and vegetarian dishes. Another group designed the itinerary for a safari supper in which they worked out the best place to take the first course, moving on to somewhere else for the main course and finally to another restaurant for pudding – all for less than £10. Each child then designed his own ideal menu.

Situations vacant

This activity originated during a topic on farming. In order to give the children a purpose for finding out about the work a farmer does, they were required to create a job description in order to compose a 'Situations Vacant' advertisement. This they did with recourse to three sources of information: books about farming, interviews with a local farmer and studies of job advertisements in the local paper.

> ## GRASSLAND FARM
>
> **Wanted : Farm Worker**
>
> Age between 16 and 30. Must have an interest in animals and must know something about them. Should not mind working long hours.
>
> **Salary: £75 a week**
>
> **Apply to:** Mr Best
> Grassland Farm
> Beccles
> Suffolk

Their various advertisements were then posted on the classroom wall. Each member of the class then applied for the job they fancied, the applications were screened, short lists produced, interviews undertaken and finally appointments made.

It might be argued that to base a programme on adult models is misleading because the society to which we belong is increasingly dissuading us from reading. There is some evidence of this being the case: television and the telephone have become popular alternatives to reading newspapers and letters, and the words 'windscreen wiper', 'choke', Keep Left', 'Ladies' and 'Gentlemen' have been replaced with little pictures on car dashboards, road signs and toilets. It has even been suggested that we learn to read and write in order to pass examinations in order to get a better job that provides a secretary who does all the reading and writing for us!

On the other hand, there is evidence to suggest that literacy is still important. Maxwell (1977) in his study of 37 rural and urban occupations found that 90% required some form of reading comprehension, 54% interpretative reading, 11% evaluative reading and 97% of jobs used manuals and books. Of course, with increased unemployment, these figures may have become redundant, though presumably one of

the responsibilities of education is to equip people with a fair chance of obtaining those jobs which are available. Also, to reduce reading to the mere vocational is to devalue a potentially varied and flexible ability. One would hope that increased leisure time might at least bring with it the opportunity for more recreational reading, for mending motorbikes with the help of manuals, for following recipes, or, like Barry Hines' *Kes* for making use of the reference library to extend and deepen knowledge.

As far as one can tell, though books may be superseded by other media for communication, information technology increasingly demands the ability to read – even if it is from a VDU!

Reading opportunities

One of the problems which besets all teachers is finding sufficient time to devote to certain activities. Reading is in competition with all other areas of the curriculum which need also to be explored and with other abilities and disciplines which need to be developed. However, there are some activities which commonly feature in the classroom that might well be sacrificed in favour of more beneficial work. I have already suggested that the excessive time often devoted to listening to children reading might be reduced, as might the administration of reading tests and comprehension exercises.

However, a special case can be made anyway for reading since it services almost every other area of the curriculum and provides a vital tool for learning. Along with other forms of vicarious experience, including television, reading provides the opportunity to extend children's experience beyond their own environment. Books are a particularly compact, convenient and accessible resource for overcoming the limitations of space and time. We don't need to fly to South America to discover what life is like in Brazil, and we can find out about the Tudors of some 400 years ago by taking from the shelf a whole history which will fit into a pocket and can be read anywhere.

And yet, opportunities for children to practise reading may be at a premium. Maxwell (1977) in his investigation into Scottish schools dealing with 8–15 year olds, found that:

> teachers gave *ad hoc* help to pupils in the use of reference books, but there appeared little systematic guidance given to pupils on the reading and study techniques required to make the most effective use of their time and efforts. (p. 51)

D.E.S. (1978) maintained that though children in the primary schools they studied were being encouraged to read fiction, '. . . in rather fewer classes they appeared to use books with ease and confidence as a source of information' (p. 47). H.M.I., in their study of 80 first schools in England (D.E.S., 1982) found that:

> in only a minority of schools the older children were encouraged to use books for finding answers to their questions in connection with topics and displays in order to extract information and compare ideas. (p. 5)

H.M.I. were similarly critical of the paucity of reading for information opportunities being offered in 9–13 middle schools (D.E.S., 1983) citing the preponderance of comprehension exercise work 'which did not allow children to consider wider, deeper issues or to explore relationships between the passages' (p. 56). I.L.E.A. (1985) in its report *Improving Primary Schools* maintains that:

> there is rarely a need for specially prepared comprehension exercises: they seldom require children to judge what matters in a passage or to read between the lines and we have met some children so adept at them that they manage to answer the questions without reading the passage through. (pp. 25–6)

Most recently, D.E.S. (1985) in its survey into 8–12 combined and middle schools found that:

> in about half the schools attention was paid to the development of extending reading skills, particularly the confident use of reference books, though in a majority of these cases the skills were practised in isolation from work in other areas of the curriculum. . . . Generally, opportunities for children to use a wide variety of sources was limited. (p. 47)

It would appear that the uncertainty which characterised much work done on early reading extends also to reading development. The next section considers what reading comprehension involves and the purposes for which reading might be used.

Comprehension and reading purpose

Many attempts have been made to analyse reading comprehension according to its various possible sub-skills and stages. Such models as the ubiquitous Barrett Taxonomy, the acronomic SQ3R and other descriptions of procedures for approaching texts, though intriguing and ingenious, do little to assist in planning classroom practice. Indeed, the same piecemeal effect which beleaguers many early reading programmes also inhibits reading comprehension as soon as it is presented according to its constituent skills or stages. Programmed learning kits such as the SRA Reading Laboratory, Reading Routes and Reading Workshop, all of which perpetuate a skill development approach, do little to help children appreciate the overall purposes for which reading can be used. In order to make their reading effective, children need to bring all of

Before reading this book, I understood comprehension — now I'm not sure what understanding means!!

their expertise simultaneously to bear, and preferably in realistic study situations rather than in the contrived conditions favoured by reading laboratories and exercises. In other words, reading skills are interdependent and reading involves the simultaneous operation of all comprehension skills, so that while the sub-skills might contribute towards comprehension, they do not represent comprehension per se. When one skill is isolated from the rest, it is no longer the same skill.

Lunzer and Gardner (1979) describe the process of reading as 'holding a conversation with the text'. Reading they claim, is a unitary activity in which the reader attempts 'to penetrate beyond the verbal forms of the text to the underlying ideas, to compare these with what one already knows and also with one another, to pick out what is essential and new, and to revise one's previous conceptions' (p. 38). The most important ability required, they propose, is the ability to reflect on what is being read.

An eclectic approach

Amongst the attitudes which need to be dispelled are the ideas that one text contains all there is to know on a given subject or that everything that is contained in a text is necessarily accurate.

One method of assessing the reliability of a text is to compare it with other texts on the same subject to see if there is conflict of ideas. This is quite a difficult task because it involves looking at several texts and either memorising the main points or making notes in order to make a comparison. However, there is a way of simplifying this process for children by making use of a photocopier. This is done by the teacher identifying a topic to be studied by the children and collecting four or five books which contain information on the topic. Then photocopy short extracts on the topic from each of the books, cut the extracts out and paste them together on one sheet being sure to acknowledge the author, book title and year of each source.

This sheet can now be used as a source of information for the children's use. By having juxtaposed the various sources together it is now much easier for the children to spot conflicting evidence.

Incidentally, this procedure does not contravene the laws of photocopying which allows one to make a single copy for research purposes.

The notion of children collecting together information and reorganising it in some way has much potential for use, not only in developing children's ability to use reading and texts to suit their own purposes but also to assist children in appreciating the eclectic nature of reading – that information can be gathered from a variety of sources.

Organising and arranging information

Here is an example of a piece of work produced by a pair of eight year olds. They set about finding out from an encyclopaedia on cold-blooded animals which creatures are potentially harmful. In order to do this they sifted through the various sections of the book noting down the name of the creature and in what way it is harmful. As their list grew they realised that a pattern was emerging – that animals are harmful in various different ways. Subsequently, they reorganised and arranged the information they had found in table form.

HARMFUL COLD-BLOODED ANIMALS

BITE	STING	INJECT	
ant	wasp bee	mosquito	INSECTS
octopus lobster shark eel	lionfish jellyfish	leech backswimmer	UNDERWATER CREATURES
crab crocodile	scorpion		OTHERS

In their book which makes suggestions for the assessment of pupils' reading strategies, Fyfe and Mitchell (1985) describe how they elected to base their model on the examination of reading tasks rather than on reading skills. They suggest two reasons for rejecting the reading skill approach. The first is that no one analysis of reading skills has yet received general acceptance. The second reason is that in the classroom, reading seldom occurs in isolation but rather features along with other modes of communication, so that teachers do not plan their work just in terms of reading skills. The term 'reading tasks' refers to what 'pupils are actually asked to *do* with texts during school work' (p. 4). They go on to claim that 'pupils' difficulties lie not only in misunderstanding texts but also in misunderstanding what they have been asked to do with them' (p. 5).

Fyfe and Mitchell describe the following three reading tasks:

1. Search-do tasks

These are the sorts of activities which involve the reader in searching for information within a text. In some cases the search phase may be the main element of the task, for example when using a dictionary to check on the spelling of a word. In other cases the search phase may be followed by a doing phase – for example, when making use of a telephone directory. Though understanding is involved here, it is more to do with understanding the nature of the task than understanding the information itself.

2. Comprehend-do tasks
Here the aspects relating to understanding have more to do with the text itself, where the reader has to comprehend and either learn – commit to memory, or store – commit to note form, part of the content. As a result of the reading, an action response may be required as in the case of using instructions, directions or filling in forms.

3. Comprehend-personal response
In this type of reading task readers are required, not only to comprehend the text but also to evaluate, to comment and to relate to their own experience.

Though the different categories are separated here, there are some tasks that are heavily weighted on several elements. For example, making effective use of an encyclopaedia may involve searching and then comprehending.

The emphasis in this form of classification is on what readers do with various tasks rather than on the sub-skills that are thought to be used to perform them. The assessment which Fyfe and Mitchell prescribe is based on the reader's ability to handle various types of text.

Robinson (1977) also questions the use of a piece-by-piece approach to reading through sub-skills and suggests that reading comprehension is 'the difference between what someone knew about a topic prior to the reading and what he or she winds up with or possesses following the read' (p. 60). Hewitt (1979) describes this prior knowledge as the reader's 'script' and suggests that what we comprehend in reading is as much a result of the application of prior knowledge as it is the effectiveness of reading comprehension per se.

Neville and Pugh (1982) argue that to describe reading as merely information gain is not enough. They maintain that reading 'changes in subtle ways the organisation of information in the reader's mind' (p. 9). The suggestion is, then, that in effective reading, readers invest something of themselves into the experience. In this way, reading becomes an active rather than a passive process in which readers engage in a kind of dialogue with the text and the author. Much of the reading undertaken in classrooms is merely an opportunity for children to reproduce extracts of the original text in their written work. Admittedly, their results are often neat and correctly presented, but there is no sense in which they

are actively involved in reading of this kind. By copying, the children are only skimming the surface of the text; they are not, as the Bullock report would urge, giving themselves any opportunity to interrogate it.

Such interrogation manifests itself for example, when the readers question the text, or express agreement or disagreement, accept, reject or relate what is being read to their own experience. For example, to accept the sentence *London is the largest table in Epping* is clearly to respond to the text at a very superficial level. A child might even read the sentence aloud with the appropriate intonation and expression and yet still not appreciate its implication. Unless the reader gains access to the meaning of the sentence and thus refutes this statement and its implication, then the activity can hardly be described as true reading, and certainly not with comprehension. Yet it is often at this surface level that children are allowed, even encouraged, to respond to texts. Southgate et al (1981) appeal for a move away from reading as a mechanical process to reading as a thoughtful process in which the reader 'contributes his own experiences and thoughts to the problem of reading' (p. 23).

Prereading plan

A useful strategy for harnessing children's scriptal knowledge is suggested by Judith Langer (1981) in her prereading plan, – 'PReP'. As well as improving the efficiency of children's reading by encouraging them to make use of their prior knowledge, Langer maintains that this strategy also assists teachers in assessing the nature and level of children's response and in making best use of a reading opportunity.

Prior to the pupils studying a particular passage, the teacher discusses its content with a small group. This prereading stage consists of three phases:

1. The teacher selects a key concept from the passage and asks the children to explain anything that comes to mind about it.
2. The teacher asks what made the children think of their response to the first question.
3. The pupils are asked whether, based on the discussion, they have any new ideas about the original concept.

As well as giving the pupils a chance to elaborate their knowledge on the content prior to the read, this prereading session also gives the teacher a chance to monitor the extent of each child's knowledge on the subject and hence to judge the extent of help they might require in studying the text. For example, a pupil with much prior knowledge on the subject may well be able to study the text independently, whilst those with some or little knowledge may require some personal guidance or direct instruction.

Perhaps the prime culprit and exponent of thoughtless reading is the comprehension exercise in which a passage or extract from a book is presented to the reader with a collection of questions afterwards to be answered. Sometimes the questions are framed in ingenious ways making use of various skills and forms of comprehension. However, such activities present all sorts of problems and really do very little to promote reading as a purposeful, realistic and thoughtful activity.

To begin with, equipped with their own 'scriptal knowledge' readers are often able to answer the questions without recourse to the text. In fact, the very nature of questions requiring inferential comprehension encourages the readers to deduce and thus bring their own experience to bear in answering the question. This makes any sort of assessment of reading through the use of comprehension exercises very difficult since one can never be sure whether a correct response is as a result of the reader's ability to extract the information from the text or whether it was something the reader already knew. Indeed, it is often possible to answer comprehension questions correctly without understanding what the text

means at all. McCall and Palmer (1983) offer the following example to illustrate this point:

> The jerrybobs impleeded hobdontily on
> the zapdons.
>
> Who impleeded on the zapdons?
> Where were the jerrybobs when they impleeded?
> How did the jerrybobs impleed?

Because, in comprehension exercises, the questions are set, they do not encourage readers to ask their own questions in pursuit of the interrogation of the text; in fact, they obviate the need to do so. Nor are comprehension exercises able to accommodate each reader's scriptal knowledge since it is impossible for the compiler, even if it is the teacher, to know the nature and extent of each child's knowledge on the subject. The result is that inevitably work on comprehension exercises perpetuates only a passive response and does little to promote the idea of reflective, thoughtful reading.

Finally, there is little evidence to suggest that children are able to transfer skills acquired through such comprehension work, to work in other areas of the curriculum. In other words, children might become proficient at doing comprehension exercises but are not necessarily developing the ability to apply their comprehension skills.

It is often argued that children need to be prepared for an examination system that still uses the traditional comprehension test question. However, I would suggest that the best preparation for such comprehension questions is not to practise doing exercises but to practise reading. In other words, confidence with reading will in itself equip the candidate for performing confidently on comprehension questions.

Grid systems

A useful alternative to the writing of answers to comprehension exercise questions is offered by the use of grids on which readers can record their findings.

	coniferous	deciduous	evergreen	soft wood	hard wood	Things made from timber	NOTES
Oak							
Ash							
Scots Pine							
Larch							
Willow							

The grid may be prepared by the teacher, though once the children become accustomed to the idea they may well be able to prepare their own grid to suit the topic on which they are working.

In this example the grid is completed by simply inserting ticks in the appropriate boxes, or by writing single words in the column labelled 'Things made from timber' and brief notes in the final column. In order to assist in this, the children refer to various sources in order to collect the information.

When the grid is completed, the children can then compose their own sentences based on the information contained in it.

This device has several advantages:

1. It facilitates an eclectic approach by enabling children to collect information from a variety of sources.

2. Since children may be able to complete some of the grid from their own prior knowledge on the subject, it enables them to combine scriptal with newly acquired knowledge.
3. By leaving some spaces empty down the left-hand column, this grid enables the readers to make their own contributions to designing the reading task and encourages them to ask their own questions.
4. The technique effectively introduces children to the valuable skill of note-taking – for example, organising and recording information.
5. Because the sentences which the children finally write are based on the information contained in the grid rather than on the original texts, the writer is prevented from copying.

Style in reading

We now turn our attention, for a while, to another activity in which we might engage, that of locomotion achieved by placing one foot in front of the other, transferring weight and repeating the procedure with the other foot leading, etc., etc. There are several words that can be used to describe this activity: marching, strolling, ambling, rambling, hiking, pacing, striding, strutting, trudging, sauntering and, of course, walking.

There is a strange anomaly in the English language which offers in excess of eleven words to describe the various styles of this relatively straightforward activity and yet allows only one word to describe the relatively complex forms of the activity – reading! So far in this book, for example, this one word has been used simultaneously to describe reading to enjoy a story, extract information, evaluate a text, recite aloud, study silently, follow instructions, savour a novel, obey road signs and answer advertisements. In other words, the one activity described as reading in fact comes in many different forms and demands of the reader a different style of reading for each occasion. The style that we adopt is determined essentially by the purpose of the read and the nature of the material being used.

Though this proposal may seem flippant, it does have important implications for the way that we promote reading to children in schools. Because there is only one word available, children may well regard the task of reading as always being the same. At its worst, this may mean standing at the teacher's desk reading aloud, or working one's way through the reading scheme; children often have a very limited view of what reading can offer them. In order to dispel this limited view of reading it is most important that we expose children to many different types of reading material, activities and situations in order to alert them to the idea that reading requires various styles of approach.

This means that children need to be able to adapt their reading style according to the nature of the text being used and the demands of the task being undertaken. In order to be efficient readers, children need to be flexible. They should be able to vary their rate, to change their style and to adapt their strategies according to their puposes for reading and the type of material being read. Such reading flexibility cannot be achieved through the use of specially contrived programmes and text-books. If anything, children need more exposure to reading materials that are not specifically written for them and more opportunities to use such materials in ways for which they were designed.

Approaches to reading for information

The 'language across the curriculum' movement puts the onus on all subject teachers to take responsibility for this within their own work. However, in secondary schools particularly, this has proved difficult as a result of the diffuse nature of the work being undertaken in the various

subject areas and also because of the problems of coordination amongst the numerous teaching staff involved. As a result, many schools have built study skill work into their programmes of pastoral care (see, for example, Hamblin, 1981, and Schilling, 1984).

On the other hand, primary schools offer a more conducive environment for incorporating study skill and reading development work into the regular curriculum. Because one teacher is usually responsible for most areas of the curriculum it means that reading opportunities can arise more readily and naturally out of normal classroom work. In particular, the provision of social science type integrated topics provides the opportunity for reading work to be undertaken *in situ* amongst genuine learning experiences.

Most class teachers seem well aware of the values offered by topic approaches and are keen to incorporate such work into their classroom activities. This is no easy task; teachers are obliged to depart from programmes and schemes and to venture further afield in their search for suitable materials. Having gathered together a collection of books, brochures, posters, manuals and magazines, the prospect of what to do with them all can be even more daunting, especially if, in other areas of the curriculum, one is used to relying on prescribed and structured programmes and books for guidance. One temptation then, is to take the resources that have been assembled and to apply a structure to them. This is often achieved by the use of work cards featuring questions for the children to answer when referring to each book. Though most carefully composed and beautifully presented using coloured card, lamination and the occasional picture, these are invariably no more than camouflaged comprehension exercises. The children soon recognise these cards for what they are and become bored.

An opposite reaction to the formidable prospect of accommodating so many books, resources, children, ideas and interests into one topic package, is to allow children complete freedom to pursue their own interests and to use the materials as they will. After all, such a democratic approach is consistent with the child-centred philosophy and seems to satisfy the pleas for child autonomy! Unfortunately, the result is invariably a vague and haphazard learning experience for the children in which they become confused and frustrated and finally resort to copying texts.

The suggestion, often proposed, that what is required is therefore a 'structured freedom' is also less than helpful. Nor would I recommend a combination of the above two approaches, for neither exercises nor copying are helpful in developing children's reading. Instead, it may be more helpful to examine the topic in question and to consider what activities the work could possibly generate. The books and resources can then be used to assist in the development of these activities. Ideally, of course, the activities should be such that they will not only interest the children but will also provide them with the opportunity to be involved in realistic and authentic, even if simulated, situations. For example, for a topic on birds, the children could be involved in designing and building a model wild-life sanctuary. They would need to use books in order to find out what sorts of habitats and conditions each breed of bird requires. This information can be stored and used as a basis for an information brochure which is given to visitors to the model sanctuary and also for the name boards and descriptions which are mounted next to each bird's reserve. Rather than simply answering questions from books, a topic about Europe, for example, could involve the children in setting up a travel agency for which they would need to refer to books in order to be able to publish holiday brochures and posters. A topic on aspects of health could include the setting up and running of a medical centre in the classroom, and so on. In these examples, the activities supply the *direction* for the topic, the teacher's task is essentially to start the ball rolling, to guide the children making sure that they are supplied with the appropriate materials and resources and to provide assistance, advice and suggestions when appropriate.

Of course, the appropriate choice of topic is paramount. The problem with many topics is that they are too academic in nature and offer very little in the way of relevant and meaningful experience for the children. Although one of the benefits that the reading experience has to offer is that it takes us outside the limits of our everyday experience, this is not to say that topics should deal with subjects that are remote. Worst of all are those topics which can best be described as 'quaint' – the sort of approach which implies that eskimos live in igloos and Red Indians in wigwams when neither has lived like that for years!

The problem is that there is a danger of the development of the processes and skills of reading taking priority over the choice of topic. For reading topics particularly, it is the area of study which concerns the children rather than the benefits in terms of skills that they might derive from it. 'To sacrifice present interest for future gain is always a chancy business' maintains Roberts (1984). 'Not only may the interest never be rekindled, but even if it is, there is no guarantee that the skills acquired will be seen as relevant and brought into play' (p. 10). Amongst the topics which Roberts describes as being those satisfying the requirements of 'real life research' are: 'Selecting a national football team', 'Planning a holiday' and 'Tracing the Blackwell Tunnel'.

Two further problems arise in undertaking topic work with children. One is in making sufficient allowance for the various reading abilities which are almost bound to figure amongst any one class of children; the other is the age old problem of preventing children from copying chunks of text.

Often, during topic work, the poorer readers are reduced to tasks which are watered down versions of what other children are doing, require very little thought and are therefore of limited use. For example, such children may be asked to draw the pictures or perhaps copy down answers given by the teacher. Wilson and Gunning (1983) suggest the following approaches for making better use of the abilities of poorer readers.

1. Break the task down into easy stages.
2. Reduce the scope of the task.
3. Do some of the task for the children – for example, write part of a sentence down for the children to complete.
4. Use forms of written language which are more parsimonious – for example, advertisements.
5. Make use of pictures as sources of information.

This last suggestion is particularly valuable, especially if one accepts the maxim that a picture speaks a thousand words. Certainly, many better readers are often reluctant to make use of illustration as a potential source of information (see Pearson, 1984). An over reliance on the text, particularly if the work is being carried out with the use of just one book, invariably results in the second problem – that of children copying from texts.

Copy writing serves very little purpose, save possibly for improving children's handwriting; it is possible to copy out a text without having any idea of the message that is being conveyed. Yet the reasons for children being tempted by copying are quite obvious. Children are well aware that they are novices at the game of learning and that they are unlikely to be able to produce something as good as an original version produced by an expert. If they copy, the result is likely to be a neat, error free manuscript which looks nice, appeals to their parents and is less likely to attract the attention of the teacher's red pen!

The causes of the copying syndrome are a lack of direction when the task was set, a lack of understanding of the purpose for reading and the excessive demand we place on children. Children copy because they need to make the task manageable; to simply ask them to 'find out about ships', for example, is too daunting a task. This is particularly so when they are expected, not only to read the information but also to absorb it, recompose it and then transcribe it. Smith (1982b) demonstrates how even adults are often not expected to fulfil all of these roles at once. He cites the case of the business executive and the secretary. Through the use of shorthand or a dictaphone the executive composes the letter by dictating, then the secretary transcribes it. In other words they share the writing task. The executive is freed from the demands of having to write and so can concentrate on the composition; the secretary need not be concerned with the ideas and so can concentrate on spelling, punctuation and presentation.

This distinction between composition and transcription in writing is a useful one and indicates how, with children, we might break the task down for them. For example, an effective way of preventing them from copy writing is to stop them from writing at the recording stage. Rather than recording their findings through the medium of the written word, the two eight-year-old children quoted below decided to consolidate their work on the post office by conducting an interview in which James plays the part of a sorting office foreman.

JANE: What sort of railway line do you use to get your post around?

JAMES: Well normal ones what passengers go on but we have our carriages to put letters on.

JANE: Does, like every post office . . . does it send their post to one certain area? Does it have like lists of where they send their post to?

JAMES: No . . . um . . . well, you just . . . er . . . um . . . . You, well, they're sorted out and then they've got certain sacks for different countries and towns.

These two children used books for their source of information, but the reason that they were not tempted to copy was that the purpose given to them of composing an interview obliged them to transpose the words read into their own words. The process of transposition alleviated the need to copy, or rather, it prevented the children from copying.

Transposition may take several forms. For example, from a text which describes the appearance of a Viking house the child could be asked to describe how the house was built; a text which describes the work of a combine harvester might be transposed into an advertisement giving the details of one such machine for sale. Another form of transposition is simplification. In the example below, Richard prepared a booklet on wild flowers suitable for consumption by an infant child. In order to do this he had to be aware of the audience for his writing and found that the texts he studied were too difficult for a six-year-old to read. So, instead of copying, he rewrote the text in simplified form.

> Flowers have pretty bits called petals.
> The petals have bright colours.
> These are so that the bee will want
> to visit the flower.
> The bee collects pollen and makes honey.

> Richard aged 9 for Debbie aged 6.

There is much potential in encouraging children to produce their own sources of information. Such opportunities are useful, not only for directing children's writing by providing audience and motive, but also as a way of developing reading and language abilities. Wade and Cherrington (1985) describe the different types of talk which might result from children working together or with the teacher on producing information books as well as the reading possibilities of locating and using sources of information, developing reading strategies, comprehending and organising information. Broderick and Trushell (1985) worked with ten-year-olds using a word processor to assist with their writing of information leaflets. They suggest that this work enabled the children to interrogate the texts and organise their composition in a way that was more effective than with normal writing. 'The children were motivated to read the text carefully, to edit and revise, to select and to focus (pp. 34–5).

An example of a topic approach

Before describing a topic undertaken with a class of second-year junior children, here is a summary of the main points made above which seem to me to be essential ingredients for topic work and which serve as objectives for such work with children.

Objectives for reading in topic work

1. To provide purposeful, relevant and enjoyable reading experiences.
2. To develop children's confidence in reading.
3. To provide practice in locating relevant sources of information.
4. To expose children to a range and variety of type of reading material.

5. To help children appreciate the uses to which various sources of information can be put.
6. To promote, as far as is possible, silent and independent reading.
7. To encourage children to read critically and evaluatively.
8. To encourage children to vary reading style according to purpose.
9. To encourage children to ask their own questions.
10. To make provision for children to read reflectively.
11. To avoid the use of comprehension exercises.
12. To encourage children to combine scriptal with new knowledge.
13. To make provision for children to organise information and make notes.
14. To assist children in being selective in their use of source material.
15. To provide structure and direction whilst making allowance for freedom and independence.
16. To make allowance for various levels of reading ability.
17. To dissuade children from copying from books.
18. To allow children to explore a variety of ways of communicating information.
19. To provide audience and direction for children's writing.

The topic

The subject of the topic outlined here was 'Houses'. Work on this topic was designed to last for four weeks, though in fact one component (The estate agents) continued for longer than that. The class of 30 second-year junior children was organised into four groups of either six or eight children. Each group contained children of mixed ability.

Since it is not possible to explain every detail of the work undertaken, five aspects of the topic are described here:

   a. Individual and pair work
   b. Group projects
   c. Developing access work
   d. The estate agents
   e. Other activities

Each of these is explained in turn, though they were all taking place simultaneously during the duration of the topic.

a) Individual and pair work
The individual work that the children produced was stored in a loose-leaf folder made for each child at the start of the project. In addition to

their own work, each folder contained some work sheets for the children to complete. These were all concerned with some aspect of 'Houses' and were designed essentially to provide opportunities for children to gather, reorganise and record information from various sources. These sources included reference books, posters displayed around the classroom, brochures acquired from estate agents and builders and D.I.Y. manuals and handbooks.

The children were encouraged to work in pairs on the folders. In this way it was felt that they would be more inclined to cooperate: to discuss the tasks and to share their knowledge and expertise.

Here are some examples, reduced in size, of the work sheets contained in the folders. The children complete the grid with details of each person's house from the information provided in the sentences. In the 'Who Says What?' sheet, the children insert appropriate job titles in the caption boxes and write words in the bubbles which each person might say as a part of the job.

WHAT ARE THEIR HOUSES LIKE ?

	Type of house	Number of bedrooms	Type of heating	Description
Betty				
John				
Kate				
Steven				
Robert				

Betty's house is like the one described on page 7 of O.B. Gregory's book <u>Houses</u>. John's house is similar to the one on poster 9.
Kate's is like the house being sold in Cotmer Rd by Ellingtons Estate Agents. Steven's bungalow is like those we saw being built on Sunnydale Estate. Robert's is similar to the one that Mrs Taylor lives in.

Some of the pairs also undertook to write a set of instructions on one aspect of home maintenance and repair. These included tasks such as 'How to lay a lawn', 'How to replace a pane of glass', 'How to lay paving stones' and 'How to construct book-shelves'. In order to help them with this, I photocopied extracts from four different home maintenance books dealing with each of these topics and mounted them together on sheets of paper – one sheet for each task. From each of these sheets an overhead transparency was produced so that, using the overhead projector, the children could scrutinise the four accounts dealing with their own task. In this way, the children soon realised that the different sources gave conflicting advice; by seeing the four accounts juxtaposed together, these differences became more apparent than if the children had been required to thumb through the four volumes separately. As one child remarked 'Which one are we supposed to believe?' The children deliberated over these accounts and finally produced their own versions of how to undertake the various household tasks. We eventually used the instructions given in one of these manuals to attempt to lay some paving stones outside the classroom.

b) Group projects

Each of the four groups was assigned one sub-topic within the main topic to explore. They were to find out all they could about this topic with a view to eventually communicating their findings to the other three groups. The four sub-topics had one thing in common, they all took a historical look at the design and construction of houses and the sorts of conditions in which their inhabitants lived.

The sub-topics used were The Tudors, The Romans, The Vikings and The Normans. The deciding factor behind the selection of these four topics was that I had just found several film strips featuring life in these times from various viewpoints. A group of parents kindly offered to convert these strips to slide form and each group worked towards producing a slide show with commentary.

c) Developing access work

In order to help the children with their research work and with a view to using the opportunity to develop their access skills, several activities and strategies were employed. Some of these were initiated a fortnight or so before the topic started in preparation for the work. During this preparation time many of the books on houses which we were going to be using were collected together in the classroom along with the posters, brochures, manuals and handbooks.

Index cards

We agreed that it would be useful to produce a catalogue of some of the subjects which we would be wanting to investigate. This would then save time and effort in locating information during the topic itself. The children worked in pairs, each pair being given a subject within the topic – for example: architects, plumbers, electricians, plasterers, carpenters, bricks, scaffolding, glazing, Tudor, Roman, Viking and Norman houses.

At this stage there was no need for the children to study the information; they were simply to look through the books, locate where the information was to be found and make a note of the source. The sources they used included the books, the posters and the brochures. For each piece of information they found, the children made a note of the source, the title and the page number where appropriate. Eventually this information was written on index cards, one for each subject, which were stored alphabetically in a box ready for use during the topic.

Contents pages
During their work preparing the index cards, the children soon realised
the value of the books' contents and index pages. However, to our
dismay we noticed that several of the reference books did not contain a
contents page. So, a group of the better readers set about compiling a list
of contents for those books that needed it. This turned out to be a more
beneficial exercise than I had realised for the children were having to
scrutinise passages of the text in order to ascertain what it was about so
that they could summarise the content for the list. Their contents pages
were fixed with paper clips to the books. More interestingly, after these
books had been returned to the school library, other children and
teachers noticed the new contents pages and asked us to stick them in
permanently.

Skimming and scanning
During the time of the topic I took advantage of the genuine interest
which the children seemed to be showing in the subject to develop their
powers of information location, skimming and scanning. The group
working on Tudor houses, for example, had gathered together five books
which contained some relevant information. Out of each book I selected
two sentences, direct quotations on the subject of Tudor houses. Each of
these sentences was written on a piece of card, and the ten cards were
given to the children along with the five books. Their task was to find the
quotations in the texts. They soon found that working through the book
from the beginning was too laborious and so they made use of the
contents page and also their ability to skim through the text in order to
find the sentences.

d) The estate agents
At the start of the project we collected together details of houses for sale
within a one-mile radius of the school. This information was obtained
either direct from the local estate agents or from copies of the weekly
Advertiser. We also visited a local estate agent in order to find out about
the service offered and how the office worked.

The details of the houses and their accompanying pictures were then
mounted on the display board surrounding a street map of the area.
Lengths of cotton, leading from each house detail to the map, indicated
the location of each house for sale. Remarkably, the abbreviated nature
of the jargon used in these advertisements was easily understood by the
poorer readers in the class!

A group of children set about cataloguing the 60 houses which were for sale by entering the details into a book. They decided to do this according to five criteria:

a. *Location*: the area was divided into five districts.
b. *Type*: whether detached, semi-detached, bungalow, terraced, flat or maisonette.
c. *Heating*: whether centrally heated (gas, solid fuel, oil), storage heaters, electric fires, gas fires.
d. *Garden*: large, medium, small or no garden.
e. *Cost*: less than £20 000, £20 000–£30 000, £30 000–£40 000, more than £40 000.

This information was also fed into the school computer on a data storage programme called *Factfile*. This meant that should we wish to recall, for example, a list of all the semi-detached, gas centrally-heated houses in Districts A or B costing less than £30 000, the computer would produce the appropriate details. Unfortunately, the computer was available to us for only two days a week; on other days the children used their catalogue.

When all the information was organised we were ready for the grand opening of 'Dell Estate Agents'. This was set up in the corner of the classroom complete with the map and details, the computer (when available), the catalogue, desk, chairs, a telephone and a typewriter – all the items seen in the estate agent's office we had visited.

In groups of four at a time, the children then acted out the situation. One was the salesperson, another the secretary and the other two were customers. The customers entered the office, were greeted with the appropriate words of welcome, and, having sat down, stated their requirements. Using the computer or catalogue, the salesperson selected houses which seemed to suit the customers' requirements and showed them the pictures on the display board. If a deal was clinched, the secretary typed the details on an application form designed for the purpose.

After a week we had accumulated some 30 application forms. Some of the children then set about calculating the profit which had been made, taking into account the agent's 2% commission and the overheads – rates, lighting, wages, etc. By the end of the month we had built up quite a going concern!

e) Other activities
During the topic various activities ran alongside those described above:

Visits

As well as going to the estate agents, we visited a nearby building site where we interviewed the foreman who showed us the processes involved in building a house. The foreman gave us samples of materials used which the children displayed, labelled and explained back in the class-room.

Visitors

One of the parents who was a bricklayer came in and built a wall in the classroom! Another parent was a salesman who explained the principles of double glazing and insulation.

Art

The children built a series of models, with captions, illustrating the stages of building a house. Working in pairs, some of the children tendered plans for a housing estate which could be built on a patch of wasteland near to the school.

Drama

As well as the drama work arising out of the estate agents, during our weekly sessions in the hall we acted out various situations. A building site was recreated, a community meeting was convened to consider vandalism in the area and some domestic situations with the theme 'Something went wrong' were depicted. These included some amusing scenes occasioned by leaking pipes and electricity cuts.

In addition to endeavouring to satisfy the objectives cited above, the work aimed at placing as much of the initiative as possible with the children for planning the work. In terms of encouraging independence the children were made responsible for their own learning and were involved in making decisions about the way the topic would develop. In designing the topic I tried to create a balance between structure and freedom by providing activities, like the estate agents, which had a secure base from which the children could explore, or by supplying them with a framework, like the group history projects, through which the children could create their own interpretations. Throughout the topic each child read a whole range of material for different purposes requiring varied approaches and styles of reading.

However, significantly there was no attempt to incorporate any literature, poetry or stories, directly into the topic work. This was a conscious decision and the reasons are discussed, along with other issues relating to the study of literature, in the next chapter on Reading to Create.

Chapter 3

Reading to Create

Response to fiction

This chapter deals with the ways in which literature and stories might be used to develop children's thinking and imagination, to add depth to their experiences of life and incidentally to develop their language and reading abilities. Again the point must be made that though such approaches to reading are dealt with separately here, there is much in common between this chapter and the previous chapters on introducing children to reading and reading to learn. For example, a major part of a child's induction into literacy can be achieved through the use of stories, particularly, though not exclusively, during the early stages. Secondly, though the essence of fiction is in the creative, emotional and artistic responses which it might evoke, many stories and novels feature an informative aspect as well. Similarly, so called non-fiction, if written well, exhibits an artistry and aesthetic quality not unlike many works of fiction. Having just read Bronowski's *The Ascent of Man* which is beautifully written as well as being highly informative, it is clear that the boundaries between fiction and non-fiction are not nearly as clearly defined as one might suppose. By the same token then, approaches to reading various genres of text may often have much in common with each other.

Nevertheless, it is appropriate to devote a separate section of this book to an area of reading which should play a major role in a child's personal and educational development. The chapter is entitled Reading to Create because it is important to stress that the reading of fiction in particular is an active experience in which the reader is involved with the author in creating an imagined world. When immersed in a good book, involved with the characters in a story or carried away by the events of a novel, we are reading 'as if we ourselves might be doing the writing, so that the author's act in effect becomes our own' (Smith, 1982a, p. 181). The

reader also creates in his mind those bits which the author leaves out. In recounting a story, portraying the characters or describing a scene, a writer does not tell all – much is left to the reader's imagination. A story is all the more engaging when it makes the reader responsible for some of its creation.

Benton and Fox (1985) describe reading a story as an 'imaginative collaboration between reader and author from which a secondary world is created' (p. 18), the 'secondary world' being 'an area of play activity between the reader's inner reality and the outer reality of the words on the page' (p. 5). They describe the process of reading as being like a journey during which, en route the traveller pictures, anticipates and retrospects, interacts and evaluates.

In stressing the underlying assumption that a reader of fiction is involved actively and creatively, Protherough (1983) maintains that a definition of fiction has more to do with what it does than what it is. He suggests that stories do things to people and that something happens to people when they read. In extreme cases this may involve physical or emotional responses, for example feeling sick, experiencing butterflies in the stomach, or feelings of fury, hate, horror or fear! More likely is a feeling of empathy with the experiences and emotions portrayed in the story, the manifestations of which might be observable or sometimes imperceptible.

In common with other forms of vicarious experience, for example, television and film, literature, suggests Hoggart (1983) has the capacity to subvert our view of life, to be disturbing. However, because literature, unlike other art forms, has a special engagement with language, it enables us to make *sense* of the experiences about which we read. In the Thomas Report (I.L.E.A., 1985) it is suggested that the reading of poetry and stories has many important purposes for children, including making it possible 'to introduce children, via the author's or poet's words, to experience and feelings that life has not yet presented, and act as a preparation for some experiences that might otherwise be over-whelming when they do occur' (p. 24).

Children's early experiences of fiction

In Chapter 1 it was suggested that learning to read has much in common with learning to talk and listen, and the importance of reading aloud to children as a means, not only of introducing them to reading but also as a device for helping them become readers was also stressed. Donaldson and Reid (1982) dispute the idea that reading can be made as easy as talking because, they argue, reading is essentially disembedded and thus constitutes a different language medium from speech. In reading, the learner is denied the paralinguistic devices which accompany speech and which therefore make learning to talk that much easier. However, this serves only to reinforce the importance and usefulness of reading aloud to children since this bridges what might otherwise be a gap between talking and reading. Whilst watching and listening to the experienced reader the child is able to make use of the facial expressions, manner-isms, gestures, voice qualities and tonal variations in order to make sense of what is being read.

Stories play an important part in children's early lives. In a sense, life itself is a story for them, featuring various characters, incidents and adventures strung together in a narrative sequence with themselves playing the central character. Often this story is enhanced by the verbal interjections of other characters, for example, when a mother reviews the day's adventures, explains something that has happened or provides a commentary on an event which is taking place at that moment. In juxtaposition with these real life stories children hear accounts of events which have happened to characters outside of their own direct experi-ences – of the five piggies that went to market, of the little boy who sat in the corner and ate plum pudding and of the little girl who was frightened by a spider. Such vicarious experiences are the child's first encounters with fiction.

It seems only natural then that the children's first, and hopefully early experiences of being read to should make use of a genre with which they are already familiar. Stories are important, not only for their intrinsic value, but also because they are a valuable preparation for thinking in many areas of human endeavour. For example, stories provide opportunities for following and constructing narrative sequences, for recognising cause and effect, anticipating consequences, speculation and conjecture, and an acknowledgement of human motive and emotion (Wells, 1982).

As important as learning to read is the fact that during these shared experiences of stories, whether they be purely oral or from a book, the child is learning *about* reading. Fox (1983) and Fox and Yerrill (1983) studied the content of children's own oral stories at the age of five and discovered a profound literary influence on their narrative productions. For example, they found children using literary techniques and providing a literary flavour in their choice of vocabulary and phraseology. They even discovered that children would adopt a more standard dialect and pronunciation than their own regional variations when recounting a story! Obviously, parents play an important part in introducing children to stories. In their book *Young Children Learning*, Tizard and Hughes (1984) begin their section on learning through stories with the following:

> Most professionals are convinced that it is important for parents to read to young children, in order to increase their vocabulary,

stimulate their imagination, and develop a love of books. Our observations suggested that reading stories, or, more precisely, the questions that are asked about them, may have another important function, that of helping the child to clarify her ideas. (p. 59)

The one-to-one condition afforded by such story experiences with a trusted adult provides the opportunity not only to present but also to talk about the story, to relate the occurrences to a child's own, idiosyncratic experience and if necessary to allay any fears, reservations or misgivings created by the story. Ironically though, in their investigations Tizard and Hughes discovered that story times at home 'were rarely the cosy, idyllic occasions traditionally portrayed in the media' (p. 59). For example, when given a chance to choose a book for themselves the child frequently chose one that was too difficult and thus subsequently became bored and restless. A number of the story sessions observed were instigated by mothers when the children had become tired or fractious which did not set a conducive climate to the occasion. However, the researchers do acknowledge the fact that they witnessed few sessions, and that this may have been because books and stories were linked with bedtime when they tended not to be on the scene. Nevertheless, though Tizard and Hughes found the story sessions to be less than idyllic, this does not mean that they were valueless.

In an article written for the magazine *Ideal Home*, Linda Gallard (1985) makes a very convincing case for the reading aloud of stories to children:

> In the two years that I have been a parent it has become clear to me that books and reading aloud are a much better medium of entertainment and education for children than television. My daughter makes her own preferences quite plain: the television will hold her attention for only a very short span (commercials for baby products and pet foods appeal to her; *Playschool* leaves her pretty cold) but she will sit on my lap and 'read' book after book until I am hoarse. (p. 116)

Gallard goes on to claim that her daughter's vocabulary is growing rapidly every day maintaining that many of these new words come from her reading for she would be unlikely to come across them in everyday conversation. 'I am not aware so far of any words she has learned from television except the greeting "Morning!" which Postman Pat uses when delivering letters' (p. 117). It seems that both Linda Gallard and her daughter are critical of television and do not accept it as a rival to books.

"COZY nappies are the BEST!"

Television viewing is an anti-social activity for her. The people on the screen are not 'real', she knows they are not talking to *her*, and her participation, although occasionally encouraged, is not actually required. Who wants to watch a cartoon of *Goldilocks and the Three Bears* when you can have a live performance in your own sitting room in the comfort of Mummy or Daddy's lap, with an 'action replay' facility for all the best bits?

Interestingly, in view of Gallard's comment about television commercials, Trelease (1984) acknowledges the influence of television, and particularly the impact that commercials have on audiences, not least of all children. In analysing the ingredients of such advertisements, Trelease identifies three essential components:

1. Send your message to the child when he or she is still at a receptive age.
2. Make sure the message has enough action and sparkle in it to catch and hold the child's attention.
3. Make the message brief enough to whet the child's appetite, to make him want to see and hear it again and again. It should be finished before the child becomes bored. (p. 28)

Trelease then uses this television formula as a basis of suggestions for instilling a desire for books and reading:

1. You read to children while they are still young enough to want to imitate what they are seeing and hearing.

2. You make sure that the readings are interesting and exciting enough to hold their interest while you are building up their imaginations.
3. You keep the initial readings short enough to fit their attention spans and gradually lengthen both. (p. 29)

So, we have an activity here which is valuable to children in many ways, and clearly should continue to be capitalised upon when children enter school. Exposure to fiction, therefore, is the earliest form of reading which most children encounter, and the one which hopefully will continue as a thread throughout their reading careers.

Approaches to fiction in school

In his excellent though disturbing article 'Leslie: a reading failure talks about failing', Tony Martin (1986) interviewed a twelve-year-old boy who had been a reading failure for most of his school career to date though happily, by the time the interview took place, had managed to overcome his problem. However, he talks eloquently and graphically about his early experiences of reading in school. When asked why, in primary school he couldn't read and had given up, Leslie says:

It was boring. They kept giving you the same books over and over again. That's why. I just gave up. If they couldn't give me proper books to read. (p. 50)

As Bennett (1985) claims 'It is the books themselves, or rather their artists and authors, who are the real teachers. One way or another, it is they who initiate children into the rules of the reading game' (p. 3). One of the most noticeable developments in the provision for primary and secondary education during the last twenty years has been the increase in the amount, range and variety of story books and novels available for children to read. The first requirement for encouraging in children an appetite for reading fiction must be to ensure that there are plenty of appealing books available for them to read. Through the use of classroom and school libraries, book clubs and school bookshops, and with the help of book loans from local libraries, this requirement has been met in most schools, even though many would maintain that they could always do with more books.

However, this chapter is concerned less with the number than with the quality of books available and particularly with the use which is made of them. In their first school survey, D.E.S. (1982) found that children were introduced too early to published reading schemes and that also there was 'an unduly prolonged concentration on the basic reading scheme especially for the able readers who should have been extending their skills while reading more demanding books of reference and fiction' (p. 5). They found that little use was made of library books to add breadth and interest to the children's reading.

Contrasted with this, in their survey of 8–12 combined and middle schools, D.E.S. (1985) found that the majority of schools provided well for pupils in terms of the quality and quantity of fiction by providing collections of paperback books and by making good use of local authority library services. The report goes on to say that:

> In the majority of the schools the children were read to, sometimes outstandingly well. A wide range of books was read: the teachers often chose material which children would have found too challenging by themselves but the quality of the material and the involvement of the teacher, who sometimes 'dramatised' voices, enabled children to follow and become involved in the narrative. The opportunities provided for the children to read for pleasure for themselves were satisfactory in over half the schools. (p. 7)

It would appear from this evidence, albeit limited, that there is something of a lull for many children in terms of their experience of literature during their early years of schooling, and that whilst many experience enriching reading experiences at home these are often not extended at school. Hodgson and Pryke (1985) in a survey into the styles of teaching reading in twenty Shropshire primary schools observed that

> Many of the competent six year olds in the survey were proficient readers of the materials provided by the school, but they had reading interests beyond the school which seemed to involve them more. The ten year olds in many cases were reading more at home than at school and the variety was considerable. (p. 6)

Perhaps we are too concerned at the infant stage to use books to develop reading ability rather than considering the intrinsic value offered by stories for their own sakes, and thus developing what Bettelheim and Zelan (1982) have termed an 'inner attitude' to reading and an appetite for books.

Nevertheless, it is argued here that simply exposing pupils to books is insufficient, that as teachers we have a responsibility to develop children's appreciation of stories and novels and their awareness of what literature is all about. The notion that the reading of books can be left to chance is not one that is applauded here. Nor is it considered sufficient to suppose that justice can be done to literature through ten minutes reading to the class at the end of the day, or by allowing only children who finish work early to 'get out their reading books'.

The suggestion is that children are capable of exploring novels and stories further than just a cursory read and that their enjoyment of works of literature might be enhanced through creative and recreative activities associated with fiction, and through discussion. This is not a prescription for courses in literary criticism, nor is it suggested that texts are analysed for incidences of metaphor, simile, imagery and symbolism. The intention is not to destroy children's enthusiasm for reading and it is acknowledged that enjoyment is paramount. Rather, the activities suggested here are designed to increase enjoyment whilst at the same time assisting children in their understanding and appreciation of literature.

Talking of stories

In this section on oral approaches to literature, we look first of all at story-telling and reading aloud, and then at the wisdom in getting children to talk about stories.

Story-telling and reading aloud

I worked for some years in East Africa where the tradition of oral literature and story-telling is still very much alive. This is partly because the existence of a written form of many of the languages is a recent phenomenon and still not widespread, and also because the people there are very good at telling stories and they love to talk. In this country good story-tellers are at a premium and the mainstay of oral literature tradition seems to be jokes. In a sense we have become a nation of listeners, or rather, viewers. It is perhaps significant though, that the last few years has seen the near demise even of the stand-up comedian, with the majority of humour on television being now presented in the form of situation comedy. Even so, the media is hanging on to some of its oral tradition with Radio 4's 'Morning Short Story', 'Book at Bedtime' and 'Jackanory', not forgetting the anecdotal raconteurs of the ubiquitous 'chat show'. Perhaps schools could do more to assist the BBC in keeping the art of oral literature alive.

It could be argued that there is too much listening for pupils to do in

And so, children, there was an Englishman, an Irishman and a Scotsman...

schools and that it is already teacher talk that dominates (see Galton and Simon, 1980 and Bennett *et al*, 1984). However, as the title of Bennett's book suggests, it is *The Quality of Pupil Learning Experiences* which is the key factor. If what children are required to listen to captures their interest, attracts their attention and engages their imagination, then it is worthwhile.

In Chapter 1 the value of reading big books to children as a means of developing their reading was discussed, particularly in terms of encouraging in children the ability to predict in order to develop reading fluency. If big book sessions are to be effective, though, they need to be viewed by children essentially as story times, with a strong feeling of wanting to know what happens next, of anticipation rather than prediction.

Reading aloud to children provides the opportunity to dramatise the story, to adopt the characters' voices and to highlight the humour, mystery, adventure and excitement of the author's words. Significantly, one of my most vivid memories of primary school is of our teacher, a rather stern character, reading Arnold Ridley's *The Ghost Train* to us. I can remember the whole class jumping out of their seats when, after a long and tense pause, he slammed his hand on the table. My appetite for George Orwell was whetted at the age of fourteen by the English teacher reading us extracts from *Keep the Aspidistra Flying*.

For many children, hearing stories read is the only opportunity they have to experience a whole piece of literature. This is true of young children yet unable to read, of course, but most relevant to older pupils whose reading ability does not match up to their interests and capacity to digest works of literature. Moreover, to promote an appetite for books in this way is likely also to have an effect on such pupils' reading abilities. Kingham (1986) found that by avoiding clinical approaches to reading instruction for a period of six weeks in an experiment with some fourteen-year-old backward readers in her care, and by immersing them instead in real reading opportunities with works of fiction, she was able to raise their reading levels noticeably.

Often it is inappropriate to read aloud whole works of fiction, particularly novels, to a group of children. It is useful to edit such longer works. For example, long descriptions or philosophical discussions might be omitted, parts of the story could be told rather than read, or a few tasters could be offered so that those who wish can take up the book and read it on their own.

Using taped stories

Teachers are under a lot of pressure to satisfy all the requirements of the curriculum and may feel reluctant to devote an excess of time to telling and reading stories. Taped stories are a good substitute and enable children in small groups to listen to works of fiction. Many of the published versions that abound are very good, and of course professionals have the facility to make use of sound effects, music and professional actors. Nevertheless, the stories they choose to record may not be the ones we would prefer. Though somewhat time-consuming it is nevertheless very satisfying and quite relaxing to record one's own tapes, or even to employ the voice of a willing colleague, relative or friend! Children seem to enjoy listening to a familiar voice that they recognise. Pupils from classes other than my own would greet me at playtime saying that I had just read them a story!

Another most valuable possibility is to get children to record their own stories, for consumption either by other members of the same class or for children in another, younger class.

Not all the onus for reading stories aloud needs to be on the teacher. These children in our care are the future generations of parents who, we hope, will want to read to their children. It makes sense, therefore, to encourage in them a pleasure in reading aloud. The benefits and pitfalls of getting children to read aloud have been discussed above. Here, however, other perspectives on this activity emerge – a delight in the sound of words, a salute to the author's artistry and a way of making the words on the page one's own. The author has done most of the ground work, the reader is free to concentrate on reciting and expressing the author's words.

Hayhoe and Parker (1984) describe this as a celebration and exploration of a book, though they warn that the celebration should not become a wake!

Oral presentations

It is often worthwhile giving the children an opportunity to rehearse an extract before reading it aloud, either to the class, to a smaller group, to the teacher or for recording on to tape. It is also valuable to allow the children to work in pairs or small groups on this. In which case they might want to adapt the text for their presentation. For example, picking out extracts of dialogue, or rewriting as dialogue a part of the book for themselves. On occasions they might want to accompany their rendition with music and sound effects. Such activities encourage the children not only to perform the work but also to study, understand and appreciate it more fully as well. Several versions are now published of short play scripts which the children can read together in small groups simply for the activity's intrinsic value or, if desired, for performance purposes as well.

Talking about stories

The first essential point to make concerning provision for encouraging children to discuss literature is that there may often be times when they would prefer not to talk formally at all. It is a mistake to force the issue, either for individual children, who may prefer not to respond during group or class discussion, or occasionally for the whole class. I once read John Wain's 'A Message from the Pigman' to a group of eleven-year-olds who listened attentively throughout but obviously preferred at the end to reflect silently on what they had heard. Interestingly, in the playground afterwards I overheard a group of them discussing the story quite passionately on their own. The point is that often the most valuable discussion takes place quite informally, spontaneously and rigorously without the teacher's direct influence.

On the other hand, there is a strong tendency for us to want to talk about experiences that we have either suffered or enjoyed – sometimes almost a need to do so. Either way, as teachers we need to be sensitive to the children's requirements on any given occasion and, when necessary, to adjust our plans accordingly. A second important reason for providing opportunities for children to talk about stories is that reading can be a very private, even insular activity; talking makes it a shared and sociable experience.

Our role as teachers during the leading of discussion sessions is really to enhance the children's enjoyment and appreciation of the story and to guide their discussion through what could be described as 'gut reactions' to a more penetrating and evaluative appraisal. Initially, both in terms of child development and in terms of the progress of a particular discussion with any age group, responses may begin with 'I liked the bit where . . .' or 'Wasn't it good when . . .' type comments, through anecdote sharing – 'My nan has a cat and she . . .' or 'I was frightened once when . . .', to a more objective kind of observation – 'I thought it was quite clever the way he made the characters . . .' or 'This one's a bit like that other one she wrote'. Foreman-Peck (1985) describes the need to shift from the distractions and distortions of personal anecdotal response, to a more critical search characterised by 'principled reading' – that is, the search for the exact intention of the author. She writes of the need to recognise 'literary talk' and maintains that 'a text which has no personal significance is dead for the reader, and a reading that has little to do with the text is not proper reading' (p. 205). However, since personal and anecdotal response is the reader's main way of making the text identifiable and relating to one's own experience it may be that any discussion needs to go through such stages before embarking on more literary appraisals. A discussion with infants may go little further than asking what they liked about the story, or which bits they found amusing. If a junior aged child offered the comment 'It was boring' or 'I thought it was great', I think I would want to extend the thinking a little by getting the child to consider what it was about the piece which elicited this type of response. Also, since hopefully we are concerned to develop children's writing as well as their reading, it is surely valuable to make the children aware of some of the devices and approaches used by

the authors we consider to be worth reading. This may help to provide a foundation upon which children's own writing can be developed.

In any event, question and answer sessions led by the teacher need to avoid a testing flavour and should be rather a sharing of the delights of the story either with the whole class, a smaller group or during individual reading conferences. This might include pointing out aspects of the story which made an impression, comparing it with other stories, and creating a connection between the author's intention (such as it is apparent) and the children's response.

Small group discussion

Some most fruitful and illuminating talk can arise from children in the absence of the teacher. The value of informal chatting about books and stories has already been considered, but setting up small group discussion in the classroom can also be beneficial. The very nature of discussion enables a group, through interaction, to pool ideas, knowledge and experience and to take consideration further than an individual's thinking might otherwise allow. However, it is useful to provide the group with some indications to direct their discussion. These could include asking them to conjecture what they think might happen next in the story or to consider what the outcome for the different characters is likely to be. Alternatively they could be asked to fill in parts of the narrative or description which are not made explicit in the text, or to fabricate information about a character based on available evidence provided by the author.

In the following example a group of four eight-year-olds are discussing *The Wolves of Willoughby Chase* by Joan Aiken. The story is in the process of being read to them in serialised form. They have been provided with a set of five questions to guide their discussion:

JAMES: 'What do you think Mrs Brisket did when she discovered that Bonnie and Sylvia had escaped?
(PAUSE)
Call the police.

REBECCA: Most probably . . . real mad.

NICOLA: Yeh, she would have gone bonkers.

REBECCA: Yeh.

JAMES: Yeh.

NICOLA: She would be ever so cross.

REBECCA: What about the cheese? She'd be a bit angry.

NICOLA: She'd try and find out how they escaped.

REBECCA: How did she get the key?

NICOLA: She might . . . they might . . . she might find it.

JAMES: No, because they dropped it in the river.

REBECCA: In the middle . . . .

JAMES: In the middle of the river . . . a big river.

ADRIAN: She can swim.

JAMES: No, but she'd tell the person who's staying there, she'd tell her off.

REBECCA: Yeh, for letting them esc . . . get out.

JAMES: She'd probably say to everybody: 'If you tell me what they've done I'll give you a whole tub of cheese.'

REBECCA: And then the cheese'll all be gone.

NICOLA: She might go and find the money and . . . and buy another lot.

JAMES: (READING) Question two: 'What do you think of Miss Slighcarp? What do you think she plans to do with Willoughby Chase?'

REBECCA: What do you think of Miss Slighcarp? Urgh! She's horrible!

JAMES: Yeh, me too – she's hoorrible.

ADRIAN: Well um . . . she might um . . . sell it.

REBECCA: Yeh, she could sell it to the people for the poor.

NICOLA: Too cruel for that.

ADRIAN: Too cruel for that.

JAMES: No, she'd want money for it; she'd do it for a high price.

NICOLA: Ten million.

REBECCA: Expect she would.

JAMES: Because she wants money.

REBECCA: She'd go and tell Miss Slighcarp about the children who'd escaped.

ADRIAN: Yeh, then they'd probably get all the police out.

JAMES: Question three: 'What do you think Bonnie feels about all that has happened?'

REBECCA: Sad.

JAMES: Happy.

NICOLA: Upset.

ADRIAN: Yes, she would be.

JAMES: She should be happy because she's escaped from that horrible school.

NICOLA: Yeh, but look, she'd just found out her aunt's not very well – Aunt Jane.

ADRIAN: She's most probably real upset, I think.

NICOLA: I expect Sylvia feels upset as well, doesn't she?

REBECCA: Yeh, she probably um, glad she's, feels happy she's left that Miss Brisket.

ALL   Yeh.

NICOLA: I bet her Mum and Dad . . . and Miss Slighcarp and if the police couldn't find her anywhere.

JAMES: Question four: 'What characters do you like best in the story and why?'

NICOLA: Sylvia's all right isn't she?'

JAMES: Yeh.

NICOLA: Sylvia and Bonnie.

REBECCA: She's quiet, Sylvia, that's why.

NICOLA: I like James, he seems kind. Do you think that, Adrian?

JAMES: I like Bonnie and Sylvia because they get up to most of the stuff.

ADRIAN: I think Simon's the best.

JAMES: He's all right.

NICOLA: I like him 'cos he's helped the children to escape.

REBECCA: I like James. (LAUGHTER)

NICOLA: He's all right, ain't he?

REBECCA: Yeh.

JAMES: Question five: 'How do you think the story will end?

NICOLA: Their parents will come back.

REBECCA: They were rescued by that boat.

JAMES: Yeh, and I think that Mr Friendship will find out Miss Brisket's children weren't doing any work so she'll be kicked out of that school. They'll have a new teacher.

NICOLA: Yeh, the children will probably get Bonnie's mum as a teacher 'cos she's so posh.

REBECCA: Bonnie will probably tell her mum about Miss Slighcarp.

NICOLA: They catch . . . the police catch Miss Slighcarp . . . .

REBECCA: . . . and Mrs Brisket and tell the police about it.

JAMES: Yeh.

NICOLA: Pattern finds where the children are and she tells the police about it.

REBECCA: They should have went and told the police about it.

JAMES: Well, there'll be one thing . . . .

ADRIAN: James might go tell the police.

NICOLA: Yeh.

JAMES: Yeh. But there's one thing, it won't end happily ever after, it won't end like that.

NICOLA: No, there'll probably be another book about it . . . adventure.

JAMES: Yeh, Mr Pearson might read it.

There are several features of this discussion which are worth noting:

1. The use they make of evidence from the text to support or refute any suggestions made, for example, following the disagreement over how Bonnie feels about all that has happened.

2. The way that, on several occasions they fill in spaces left by the author, for example, in speculating as to what might have happened back in the school following the girls' escape.

3. The way that initial, spontaneous responses are then explained and refined – for example, in their appraisal of the character of Miss Slighcarp.

4. The way that the dynamics of the discussion works, with participants

picking up and expanding each other's comments. Evidence of this is apparent from the frequent use of the word 'Yeh'.

5. The way that the children project into the characters and incidents, for example, in their surmising about Sylvia's feelings.
6. The acknowledgement of certain story conventions, for example, that good is likely to win over evil but that, in James' opinion, the story is unlikely to end happily ever after.

In terms of an awareness of literary techniques there is little evidence of this in the discussion, nor is there an instance of literary criticism. However, the children's enthusiasm for the novel is very apparent, as is their understanding of the characters and the events and it would seem that the participants are learning from the discussion experience.

Approaches to fiction

In this section some approaches for the development of children's responses to fiction are discussed, including an appraisal of topic work in literature, a look at individual response, recreative activities and some ways of studying the presentation of a novel.

Topic work

Popular in schools is the topic approach to learning in which subject barriers are transcended and various activities are brought to bear in pursuit of some knowledge and understanding of subjects like Houses (the topic described in Chapter 2), Power, the Romans and so on. In an attempt to achieve integration, aspects of the curriculum are pooled and the opportunity is taken to encourage application of such abilities as reading for information, access and survey techniques, artistic depiction, dramatisation, writing, model making and anything else which is deemed possible and appropriate. This is all highly desirable and often very successful, but the place of literature in such social science type topics is questionable. For example, one may be tempted to feature Betsy Byers' *The Midnight Fox* in a topic about animals, or *I am David* by Anne Holm in a topic on Europe. However, careful consideration of the Byers novel reveals that it is less about foxes than the problems of growing up, and *I am David*, though set in and around Europe is essentially about a child's growing awareness of life. To include such novels in regular topic work is to divert attention away from the essence of the story and from the qualities of these works of art which make them creative and unique. As Fox (1974) explains 'We must remember that *Treasure Island* is not a handbook on piracy, nor is Hickory Dickory Dock about the nocturnal habits of mice'.

Rather than distorting a work of fiction so that it will fit conveniently into a topic package, we are far more likely to be able to explore the essence of the work if a topic is prompted by the novel itself. In this way activities are based around the novel rather than the novel around the topic.

Mackay and Pepin (1984) see the use of fiction topics as a means of intensifying children's experiences of books. 'The richness of language from the use of fiction' they suggest, 'can counter the barren fact-amassing characteristics of many topics' (p. 159).

Cheetham (1976) suggests that the elements of a novel that need to be explored are:

1. The story – incidents and episodes which capture the children's imagination.
2. The various characters and their relationships.
3. The relationship between people and incidents in the book and the children's own lives and experiences.
4. The physical settings and changing moods of the novel.

Cheetham goes on to suggest that:

> The work prompted by the novel should come from these elements which become the touchstones of the project; however far one may go in the creative work there must be a constant return to the novel. (p. 195)

I believe that, in addition to Cheetham's checklist, children at the upper end of the junior age range are quite capable of developing an awareness of the writer's style and means of expression. An instance of this happening is explained in the next section. Most of the activities described in the rest of this chapter are the sort that might feature in this literature model for topic work.

Individual response

Emma is eleven years old. She is keen on reading, enjoys a good story and likes talking about books that she has read. Although she may not be typical of many children in the top classes of our primary schools, she does represent a large number of avid readers who have gained an appetite for reading and whose needs should be catered for. It was felt that Emma was ready to have her appreciation of literature extended – to explore rather than exploit, her enthusiasm for fiction and to draw her attention to salient aspects of the novel and of techniques used by the author.

To this end, a copy of *The Wolves of Willoughby Chase* was prepared with questions written on small slips of paper attached strategically throughout the book. Emma was presented with the book which she was to read by herself in the normal way with the extra provision that she was to respond in writing to the questions as she reached them in the text.

Examples of the questions, along with Emma's responses, are shown below. The sample of questions and responses are presented here, not in the order in which they occurred in the novel, but according to the following categories:

a. Presentation
b. Narrative
c. Characters
d. Atmosphere and mood
e. Form
f. Language
g. Message

a) Presentation

Q: What impression do you get from the front cover?

A: It looks mysterious as though it has deep down sources of evil hidden inside it.

Q: What do you think the story is going to be about?

A: The wolves trying to capture some people, but children set the people free and send the evil away for ever. I think that it is the sort of book that will have me sitting on the edge of my seat wondering what is going to happen next.

b) Narrative

Q: How do you think the story will end?

A: In the end I think that Mr Grimshaw, Miss Slighcarp, Mr Gripe and Mrs Brisket will be arrested and punished. Then I think they will find out that Sir Willoughby and Lady Green will not have drowned but were saved. Then maybe they will all go back to Willoughby Chase and Simon and Aunt Jane will live with them and they will all live happily ever after!!!

c) Characters

Q: What do you think of the characters in the novel?

A: I think that Miss Slighcarp is magical and evil and is friends with the wolves. Mr Grimshaw is a proud, aloof man. Bonnie is gentle, kind but mischievous. Oh, I'm so cross with Miss Slighcarp, how dare she send the children away?

d) Atmosphere and mood

Q: While reading the novel where do you imagine yourself to be?

A: You feel you want to, with Sylvia, put your arms around her and comfort her. I see myself as Sylvia, wanting to help Bonnie but absolutely terrified of Miss Slighcarp.

e) Form

Q: Does the first paragraph capture your interest?

A: It sounds mysterious 'for fear of the wolves grown savage and reckless from hunger'. Isn't that an exciting sentence? The evil is really beginning to work up in the wolves, even in the first paragraph.

Q: Why does the author frequently mention people sleeping?

A: The writer describes several times when people sleep. They have uncomfortable and restless sleep in the school, but then Sylvia has peaceful and restful sleep in the cart which is so comfortable and warm. I think the writer tries to show the mood of the scene by the way different people sleep.

f) Language

Q: What do you think these words mean? Indomitably:

A: This means angrily or hateful or nervous.
remorsefully:

A: Means pitifully, regretfully.
invincible optimism:

A: This probably means that Bonnie is very determined to get away from this dump.

g) Message

Q: Does the story have a moral?

A: I don't think a story like this can have a moral. But I found it very touching and very involving.

Through being obliged to pause and deliberate over the questions Emma was encouraged to reflect on what she was reading and to think more deeply about various aspects of the novel. In this case she displays a remarkable insight into the substance of the novel, its poetry and modes of presentation. In fact Emma admitted to enjoying the writing activities and found that she discovered aspects of the novel that might otherwise have gone unnoticed. One cannot expect this method of study to appeal to all readers, nor is it one that can be used too often with one child. However, Emma found that she read subsequent novels in a different light and with renewed insight and enthusiasm. As she said some weeks later, 'I hadn't realised that books had so much to them; when I read now I seem to know the sorts of things to look for'.

This technique also provides a way, albeit lengthy, of monitoring children's reading and responses to stories. More parsimonious devices include reading cards, in which children record the books they have read, and reading reviews. To make the writing of reading reviews a compulsory result of having completed a book is, I believe, a mistake, though as a voluntary activity it can be valuable, particularly when the reviews are used for the consumption and guidance of other readers. However, the response form below is a useful alternative and it serves both purposes – a record of the books read by each child and an opportunity to monitor response. Having filled in the details at the top, the reader simply inserts ticks next to the categories they find appropri-

---

Reading response form

NAME .... DATE ......

TITLE OF BOOK ....

AUTHOR .... PUBLISHER ....

What sort of story is it?	How did you rate the novel?
comedy	interesting
adventure	boring
historical	exciting
horror	relaxing
romance	frightening
fantasy	amusing
travel	sad
....	....
....	....

ANY OTHER COMMENTS ....
....

---

ate for that book. The two spaces at the bottom of each column are for any categories that the reader might want to add and the space at the bottom of the form is for additional comments that the reader may want to make. The completed forms can then be filed away, but at the same time made available for other readers to scrutinise if they wish.

Creative and recreative activities

So far the suggestions made for responding to fiction involve readers in exploring the meaning of the text, searching for the intentions of the author and articulating their own reactions to the story. However, an important feature of fiction is in the way it is able to trigger off ideas, to make the imagination wander and to encourage the mind to create and recreate. For most of the time such imaginings are private, covert affairs which go on in the mind of the reader and never see the light of day. Often though it is rewarding to seek expression for one's responses, to make them public and overt. For example, a scene or event depicted in a novel might be acted out by a group of children or a particularly vivid description can be prepared for reading aloud with musical accompaniment. During a reading of Clive King's *Stig of the Dump*, one group of second-year junior children built a model of Stig's home based on the descriptions provided in the novel. To accompany their creation the children wrote poems describing the dump:

> Stig's dump has
> Tins and things.
> Cars and Mars
> Bar packets.
> Orange peels,
> Bicycle wheels,
> And pumps
> In Stig's dump.

The same children also staged and tape recorded an interview between Stig and a radio reporter and wrote newspaper reports covering one of the incidents in the story.

The production of documents and facsimiles helps children to appreciate the building up of character in a novel and the way that it is possible to develop a character study. Personal dossiers can be compiled containing fabricated documents: birth certificate, samples of school reports, passport with photograph, application for the job on which the character is currently working and references. In assembling a dossier on

Miss Slighcarp, for example, the children hunted through magazines to find a photograph which they felt resembled most closely their impression of the character for use in her passport.

Using this photograph approach, each group was allocated one character from the novel. They mounted their chosen photograph in the centre of a large sheet of paper and then surrounded it with words, phrases and sentences describing facets of the character which they scrawled around the picture. A graffiti effect results which captures the essence of the characters in question.

Character matrix

This activity is designed to provide the opportunity to explore characters featured in the novel. In the matrix below possible character trait dichotomies are listed in the two columns. These might include descriptions of temperament, attitude, conduct, demeanour, or indeed any aspect of people's behaviour that seems appropriate to include. Several of these grids need to be produced so that each can be devoted to one character. Working preferably in groups, the children decide where along the dichotomy the character they are studying would feature. This is then represented by a tick in one of the boxes with a brief explanation to accompany it.

NOVEL					CHARACTER	
TICK ONE BOX IN EACH LINE					**EXPLANATION**	
kind				cruel		
happy				sad		
patient				impatient		
generous				greedy		
unselfish				selfish		
polite				impolite		

The description of Mrs Brisket's school in *The Wolves of Willoughby Chase* is particularly vivid. By careful reference to sections of the novel, one group undertook the following projects:

1. A list of school rules was compiled. Some were actually mentioned in the text, others were suggested by the group.
2. Bonnie and Sylvia's school reports, though not mentioned in the text, were composed and designed.
3. Copies of letters which Bonnie might have written whilst in school were produced.
4. The front page of the newspaper published on the day when the scandal of Mrs Brisket's school was exposed, was published. This included eye witness accounts all written in appropriately journalistic language.

Other activities connected with this novel included a large cartoon strip depicting the main events of the story, each of the fifteen pairs in the class being given responsibility for one incident and frame, and a map with pictorial inserts which plotted the various locations and journeys travelled during the events of the story.

The presentation of stories

In an article which describes some work undertaken with her class of six to seven-year-olds, Davies (1985) describes how, when she invited her author husband into the classroom to talk to the children, it emerged that they had little idea how books were written and produced. They thought, for example, that the author was responsible for the whole process from start to finish, including making the paper! It would be most interesting for children to find out about the making of books; this sounds like a good subject for a topic in its own right. Perhaps the best way of familiarising children with the process is to give them a chance to write books for themselves so that they can experience the various stages first hand. The whole thing can be formalised to an extent by appointing editors from amongst the children, designers, typesetters (using type-writers), printers (using the spirit duplicator) and a publicity and marketing department. One class of children with whom I conducted a topic of this type suggested even that they should form their own branch of 'Sogat'!

It is also useful to familiarise children with the ways in which published novels are presented and some techniques used by writers in furthering their craft. Many of the children who read *The Wolves of*

Willoughby Chase remarked that the novel was hardly about wolves at all. For this reason they felt that the cover of the novel featuring a pack of wolves, and indeed the title itself, were misleading. It was suggested that the children might like to design alternative covers and invent more appropriate titles. Amongst those suggested were *Bonnie and Sylvia*, *Evil at Willoughby Chase*, *Escape and Victory* and the cleverly ambiguous *Chase Tears*. In addition to this, more illustrations were drawn and inserted into the two library copies ready to enhance the reading for future generations of Aiken fans.

A group of nine to ten-year-olds studied some of the conventions used by writers to elucidate their writing. For example, from Anne Holm's *I am David* they made a list of all sentences in the first and last chapters that finished with exclamation marks:

> Don't think! Don't think!
> Salonika!
> Go south until you reach Salonika!
> Think of nothing else!
> Salonika!
> And now he had a lift!
> Johannes!
> Never had he met such a child!
> Mamma Mia!
> And now he must take to the water!
> Suddenly he knew that he did not want to die!

. . . and from the final chapter:

> It was good to be alive!
> It was the car he had just seen at the frontier post!
> The truth, David!
> He had returned to them!
> How much he could remember in such a short time!
> It was going to take David's place!
> You shouldn't have done it!
> Run! Run!
> David, my son David!

In their own way, these exclamations capture the feelings of the novel, and of David himself; in a sense they tell the story as well – particularly conjurous for someone who has read the book. Sentences in the form of questions can be given a similar treatment and highlight key points in the story from a different perspective.

Making metaphors

One way of introducing children to the idea of metaphor is to focus attention on themselves in imagining what they might be if transformed into other objects – a sort of metaphoric metamorphosis.

The children have to complete sentences; here is one child's response:

> If I were a musical instrument, I would be a *trombone*.
> If I were an item of furniture, I would be a *wardrobe*.
> If I were an item of clothing, I would be a *boot*.
> If I were a building, I would be a *block of flats*.
> If I were a vehicle, I would be a *Volvo*.
> If I were a meal, I would be *beef curry*.

Daniel, aged 9.

The children found this activity amusing and thought it interesting the way that individuals' responses did seem to reflect their personalities.

This section on the presentation of stories has concerned itself with familiarising children with some of the craft and artistry that writers of fiction employ. By considering the writing of others and by writing themselves, children can be introduced to some of the conventions of the writing game. When studying children's writing I have noticed that they do model their efforts on the sorts of books that they have been reading. The child who writes:

> Jane is a girl. She is a nice girl. She has a red dress. She went to the zoo and saw some animals. When she came home she went to bed.

has more than likely been reading books featuring this same turgid style of writing. In other words, children write in the way that they read. Bennett (1985) observes that, in forming a bond with the author, children are able 'to see what the author/artist is trying to show them, to recognise distinctive styles and, most exciting, to make critical judgements' (p. 3).

Children model themselves, not only on authors, but also on the other children, adults and teachers around them. From a teacher's point of view, more important than providing children with original and ingenious activities, is to demonstrate to them a commitment to fiction, a love of reading and an enthusiasm for books.

Chapter 4

Problems and Assessment

Reading problems

During the Introduction to this book, it is suggested that all children have become proficient learners before they enter school, and that they continue to learn thereafter. Of course, some of the things that children learn may not be the most desirable or educationally acceptable; they may learn to daub graffiti, display defiance, smoke cigarettes or swear. Nevertheless, these activities have all been learned, and often most efficiently, too. But as with all of us, there are some aspects of learning which elude our pupils, and reading seems often to feature amongst these. There may be many causes for this: poor eyesight, impaired hearing, negative attitudes towards reading at home, stress in their personal lives, or perhaps simply tiredness and fatigue may all militate against the concentration and application required to master the intricacies of reading. Whatever the cause, a likely effect is the development of a resistance towards reading which prevents the child from becoming literate. In cases such as these, pupils are often described as lacking the motivation to read, yet interestingly most of our learning is achieved unconsciously, without our being aware that we are learning – we learn incidentally and without noticing it. And motivation is no guarantee of learning; I am highly motivated to cultivate flowers to make my garden look attractive, yet in spite of this, I still seem incapable of becoming a gardener. What is more, I seem to know the year of manufacture as indicated by car registration letters, and I didn't even want to learn that! One thing that children can learn only too easily is that they are no good at something and, what is more disturbing, they learn how to react in the face of failure.

The problem is exacerbated by the fact that remedial treatments used to assist those readers who are having problems, are often too far removed and isolated from the reading process itself. This is particularly so when diagnostic instruments are used to identify specific problem areas and weaknesses which are then treated. As children are subjected to programmes for developing either word recognition, phonic awareness or perhaps context cue use, they are likely to lose sight of the whole system and purpose for reading. Such treatment may make reading increasingly difficult for children to learn, especially when attention is focused on the children's weaknesses.

Ironically, some problems are caused for children by the methods used to teach reading. If anything, children with reading problems need more exposure than others to realistic, not clinical, reading situations, they need more guidance in the use of the whole system of reading and more opportunity to capitalise on strengths rather than weaknesses. For these children the promotion of interest and confidence is paramount.

I once watched a swimming instructor working with a young boy who had lost the use of one leg in an accident and had to walk using crutches. I noticed that in teaching the child to swim, the instructor concentrated attention on the boy's arms first and soon got him to stay afloat with the additional help of his one good leg. Rather than attempting to remedy the weakness, the instructor capitalised on the boy's strengths and, in so doing, succeeded in increasing the boy's confidence as well. For effective learning to take place, pupils need to use as much of the reading system as possible, though concentrating preferably on those aspects that they are most readily able to employ. For example, if beginner readers seem able to make use of bibliographic cues, then it is most beneficial to capitalise on this by providing encouragement and opportunity in the use of pictures for attempting to decipher the text. It would be a mistake to deprive them of such picture cues in an attempt to force them into employing other components of the cue system. Similarly, children who seem willing to relate the meaning of the text to their own knowledge and experience need to be encouraged to get straight to the meaning of the text, by being given a chance to talk about the content and by having the text read to them.

So, children learn in different ways and have their own preferred strategies for dealing with reading. By building on these preferences and by giving them a chance to tackle reading using strategies with which they are comfortable and confident, children can then be alerted to the benefits of incorporating other aspects of the cue system into their reading repertoire. Catering for differences in reading style and ability is a question of emphasis rather than kind. However, though teaching strategies may need to be varied in order to accommodate children's individual learning needs, there are approaches that will suit all learners of reading; it is such approaches that are described in Chapter 1. Of particular importance is the strategy of reading to children. The difference between slow learners of reading and those that learn readily and easily is that the slower learners need to be read to more often and for longer.

In addition to reading to children, a programme for slower learners might include the following, depending, of course, on the interests, preferences and reading strengths of the learner.

1. Reading to the children with the opportunity for them to join in when they feel able. (See 'Big Books' on page 26.)
2. A paired reading approach in which the learner takes initiative for the reading but calls upon the help of the teacher when required. (See 'Paired Reading' on page 28 and also Reading Conferences on page 92.)
3. During shared and paired reading, the learner is alerted to features of the text and is given the opportunity to practise word recognition and initial letter sounds in the context of an interesting and meaningful passage. (See 'Introducing Reading Components' on page 8.)
4. Using language experience approaches, the learners are made responsible for composing original texts which are transcribed by the teacher and manipulated, rearranged and read by the children. (See 'A language experience Approach' on page 26, and 'The D.I.Y. Book' on page 18.)
5. The children are involved in using reading as a part of their quest for information and learning. As well as providing a chance to apply their knowledge, this also helps children to appreciate a purpose for reading. (See Practical Boxes in Chapter 2.)
6. The children are involved in using reading as part of their response to fiction. There is no reason why children with reading problems need be precluded from the discussion and recreation of fiction, particularly when it concerns stories that have been read to them. (See Practical Boxes in Chapter 3.)
7. The children are given ample opportunity for the independent reading of real books. (See 'Finding the time and the place' on page 22.)

Assessing reading

If teachers are to accommodate individual children's needs they need to employ effective ways of assessing and recording children's progress.

This is no straightforward matter, and any systems which attempt to make the process simple and easy are almost bound to be missing the point. For example, it is inadequate simply to record the numbers of the books read, or which particular words have been 'learned' today. Such records are less than informative for they describe nothing of the nature and quality of the children's reading. Individual reading records should provide an analysis of reading behaviour: likes and dislikes, strengths and weaknesses, preferred strategies, responses, opinions, views and ideas.

In order to be able to record appropriate information it is necessary to assess the children's progress. The main purpose of assessing children's reading is to obtain information which will be helpful to teachers in providing an appropriate reading programme for the children. Three assessment methods are discussed briefly below: observation, reading conferences and testing.

Observation

It is surprising how much information can be gathered from watching children read, particularly during occasions when they are reading silently and independently. The amount of time that a teacher can devote to observing the children reading is obviously limited. Nevertheless, any time spent on observation is worthwhile for it is the one way of monitoring children's reading *in situ*. Since one of our aims must surely be to develop children's silent reading, then it is worth spending some time scrutinising their behaviour when reading in this way.

Conclusions reached from such observation may be only approximate, especially as it is necessary to watch in as unobtrusive a way as possible. However, the sorts of behaviours to look out for might include:

1. *Eye movement*: how quickly the eyes move across the text, whether there seems to be a lot of deliberation over individual words or whether the reader is scanning the text.
2. *Concentration*: the degree of interest and absorption in the text being read, for how long the read is undertaken without distraction, the length of time spent on one book.
3. *Distribution*: the length of time spent on each page of the book, the relationship between time spent on text and illustration, the relationship between time spent on and off task.
4. *Independence*: how much of the time is spent reading alone and how much sharing reading with others or seeking their help.

5. *Vocalisation*: whether the text is read silently, the words are mouthed or read aloud.

Such observations, even if lasting for only a few minutes, provide valuable information about children's strategies for reading and about their preference in choice of book, especially if the reading material is chosen by the children themselves during independent reading times. Records of observation can be considered alongside information on other aspects of children's reading to provide a profile of each child's reading behaviour.

Reading conferences

Listening to children reading aloud is the only overt and direct method available for monitoring children's ability to decipher texts. The term 'conference' is used here because, if reading is to operate as a collaborative activity, then teacher and pupil must work together on the reading task. Thus reading conferences should include conversation about the children's progress and discussion about the material being read. When reading aloud sessions become routine, with children taking turns in reading to the teacher on a regular and frequent basis, then the chances are that the quality of the sessions will become routine and perfunctory as well. It is more profitable for children to enjoy longer, but less frequent sessions with their teacher with the chance to deliberate over their reading, than to be subjected to a daily examination.

Arnold (1982) makes some useful suggestions for what she describes as the 'shared reading interview' which would involve more than merely hearing children read.

> Teacher reads some of the text.
> Child reads some of the text.
> Teacher sets a purpose at beginning of interview to encourage skimming and scanning to find certain elements of the text.
> Teacher asks child to read a paragraph silently first and then to read it aloud.
> Teacher asks a child to read a paragraph silently and then questions him on it.
> Teacher encourages child to ask questions about text that has just been read (either by himself or teacher).
> Teacher discusses decoding problems with child (having carried out miscue analysis in advance).

Teacher and child discuss contents of text in terms of appreciative/emotional response.
Teacher discusses child's difficulties in reading in general, attitudes, likes and dislikes and so on. (pp. 82–3)

In any event, the main aim of listening to children reading is the development of silent reading. In this respect it is important for teachers to help children during reading conferences, to provide a word when to insist on children working it out for themselves would inhibit fluency and understanding, but at the same time to alert children to the availability of the various cue systems. In terms of assessment, it is important to monitor children's strengths, as well as their weaknesses, and to examine positive as well as negative strategies. In so doing we are more likely to develop children's confidence and willingness to read.

Testing

Over the past few years, education has suffered from what can only be described as a mania for testing. Based on the psychological model of counting and measuring, attempts are made to assess children's performance using supposedly objective testing instruments. Not only this, but educational research has attempted to establish the efficacy of programmes of innovation and children's performance in various situations and circumstances has been assessed through the use of formal testing devices. Such results are almost bound to be misleading, for formal reading tests, particularly those of a normative, standardised type, can seldom be used as accurate predictors of children's actual reading performance. A reading age of 9.5 for example, provides no information about the quality and nature of a child's reading, and two children with the same reading quotient may actually read in very different ways. One twelve-year-old, non-English speaking, Portuguese boy achieved a reading age of 9.7 on the Schonell Reading Test.

Admittedly, more recent reading tests have managed to simulate much more closely the actual circumstances in which children read, and some of the items featured on these tests are ingenious and worthy of use in any classroom. However, it is by no means clear why such items need to be presented in test form, for a reading test can give no more information than teachers who know their children well can ascertain for themselves. The argument is often made that it is important to monitor local and national standards and that the only way of doing this is through normative testing. However, since it is impossible for such reading tests to accurately reflect the children's reading performance, the results are rendered less than useful anyway! The only way to become a reader is to read; the only way to assess reading is to examine reading itself, not some manifestation of it.

Throughout this book, reading is regarded as a means of developing thinking and learning rather than as a separate skill to be acquired. The content of the material most likely to capture the reader's interest and imagination is seen as more important than the processes involved in reading. In this connection, the reading activities suggested here are invariably interdisciplinary in nature and involve also activities other than reading – for example, talking, writing, reasoning, organisation, planning and design. Implied in the activities suggested is the notion that we should not impose reading on children but rather should help them to realise the potential that the printed word has to offer so that they will readily turn to reading themselves as part of their quest for learning and the development of their own experiences. Many of the ideas contained in this book were devised by children themselves and were borne out of their desire to use reading to satisfy their own needs. I feel it is important that children have an investment in the curriculum and that they are given responsibility for their own learning. It is only then that children will become readers in the fullest sense of the word.

Sources

The following reviews summarise some recent publications concerned with encouraging children to become readers. The reviews are listed under three headings: 'Learning to read', 'Reading to learn' and 'Reading to create', though inevitably there is some overlap between the three.

Learning to read

BENNETT, J. (1985) *Learning to Read with Picture Books* (Stroud: The Thimble Press, 2nd edition).

The majority of Jill Bennett's book comprises a valuable list of titles, with reviews, of publications for children which satisfy the requirements of 'real books'. In addition, some suggestions are offered for teachers on how to organise reading and run a classroom without the need to use reading schemes.

BETTELHEIM, B. and ZELAN, K. (1982) *On Learning to Read* (London: Thames & Hudson).

Bruno Bettelheim and Karen Zelan subtitle their book *The Child's Fascination with Meaning* and present a persuasive argument for rejecting any methods or materials which do not encourage children to read for meaning. They deal with such topics as 'Why children resent reading', 'Taking reading seriously' and 'Empty texts – bored children'.

BRANSTON, P. and PROVIS, M. (1986) *Children and Parents Enjoying Reading* (London: Hodder & Stoughton).

The authors describe in detail the processes by which they established a programme for parental involvement in their school. Included in the book are suggestions for ways of conducting initial briefing sessions with parents, advising parents on how to read with their children at home, running workshops and clinics to discuss strategies and problems. Also included are some original ideas for book-based activities in the classroom and several pages of attractively presented and illustrated materials such as letters, a daily comment booklet, information sheets, questionnaires and activity sheets which readers are free to photocopy.

CASHDAN, A. (ed.) (1986) *Literacy: Teaching and Learning Language Skills* (Oxford: Basil Blackwell).

A collection of articles by various writers, including Gordon Wells, Colin Harrison, Helen Arnold, Peter Brinton and John Merritt covering such topics as styles of interaction, reading and spelling, readability, children as writers, hearing children read, project work, assessment and the use of the microcomputer in reading.

HOLDAWAY, D. (1979) *The Foundations of Literacy* (London: Ashton Scholastic).

Don Holdaway is regarded by some as the originator of big books and the shared reading approach. His illustrated book provides some valuable suggestions for shared reading activities in the classroom, including some thoughts on children's writing. Particularly useful are his ideas on integrating approaches for children's reading.

LONG, R. (1986) *Developing Parental Involvement in Primary Schools* (London: Macmillan).

The book examines the rationale underlying the involvement of parents in the work and life of the school and then makes practical suggestions for workshops designed to explore such topics as the potential of parents as educators, the possible benefits and problems of parental involvement schemes and the development of home-school relations. The final section provides a list of useful reference sources on the subject.

MEEK, M. (1982) *Learning to Read* (London: The Bodley Head).

The book is intended for reading by both parents and teachers and provides a very readable account of steps taken towards reading by children before school, at five, seven and eleven years, through to adolescence. Margaret Meek concludes with lists of books which might appeal to readers of these different ages.

MOON, C. (ed.) (1985) *Practical Ways to Teach Reading* (London: Ward Lock).

This book, edited by Cliff Moon, contains accounts written by class teachers of how various aspects of reading can be undertaken in the classroom. The suggestions cover work in both infant and junior classrooms and deal with such topics as the children's contact with non-fiction, using *Breakthrough to Literacy* material, reading in a multicultural classroom and ways of promoting literature as well as reading conferences and activities for children with reading problems.

SMITH, F. (1978) *Reading* (Cambridge: Cambridge University Press) and (1983) *Essays into Literacy* (London: Heinemann).

Along with Kenneth Goodman, Frank Smith is a pioneer in the field of studies on the psycholinguistic approach to reading. Smith's intention is not to provide practical ideas but rather to stimulate teachers into examining what reading is all about. More recently, Smith has extended his writing to include a range of curriculum issues, and booklets with such titles as *Collaboration in the Classroom*, *The Promise and Threat of Microcomputers in Language Education*, *What's the use of the Alphabet?*, and *Misleading Metaphors of Literacy* are available from the Reading and Language Information Centre at the University of Reading.

TRELEASE, J. (1984) *The Read Aloud Handbook* (Harmondsworth: Penguin).

The cover of Jim Trelease's book describes it as the bestselling guide for parents, though its list of 300 stories, picture books and poems for children is obviously useful for teachers as well. Also useful are suggestions for approaches to reading aloud to children.

WATERLAND, L. (1985) *Read With Me* (Stroud: The Thimble Press).

Subtitled *An Apprenticeship Approach to Reading*, Liz Waterland's book gives a marvellous account of the way, as a teacher, she shares in the reading experience with children in her infant classroom. Included in the book is a list of some of her children's favourite picture books, a model for a 'Reading Experience Record' and some extracts from her school's booklet on reading which is given to parents.

YOUNG, P. and TYRE, C. (1985) *Teach Your Child to Read* (London: Fontana).

Another guide for parents, this book by Peter Young and Colin Tyre is one of the most enlightened of its type and gives valuable advice for introducing children to reading, writing and spelling. Chapter headings include 'Apprenticeship to Reading', 'Lap Learning' and 'How parents teach reading – side by side'.

Reading to learn

AVANN, P. (ed.) (1985) *Teaching Information Skills in the Primary School* (London: Edward Arnold).

Edited by Pat Avann, this book features a series of articles written by classroom teachers who describe approaches they have used to develop children's reading and learning. Topics covered include introducing information skills to infants and children with learning difficulties (though there is rather an overemphasis here on arranging things in alphabetical order), examples of a project approach and problem solving activities and an article on the use of the microcomputer.

FYFE, R. and MITCHELL, E. (1985) *Reading Strategies and their Assessment* (Windsor, NFER Nelson).

As well as their suggestions for the formative assessment of children's reading based on reading tasks, Ronald Fyfe and Evelyn Mitchell present some intriguing ideas for developing pupils' responses to fiction and non-fiction material. The report is based on work carried out with upper primary and secondary pupils in Scotland.

LUNZER, E. and GARDNER, K. (1984) *Learning from the Written Word* (Edinburgh: Oliver & Boyd).

This book is a sequel to the Schools Council report *The Effective Use of Reading*. In this later work, Eric Lunzer and Keith Gardner explore the use of the approach called 'DARTS' (Directed Activities Related to Texts) and present activities, with case studies, for developing pupils' abilities to analyse and reconstruct texts.

WILSON, E. (1983) *The Thoughtful Reader in the Primary School* (London: Hodder & Stoughton).

Elizabeth Wilson presents some ideas on the constituents of thoughtful reading and the strategies and attitudes needed by effective readers. These are based largely on the Open University's model of literacy. Examples are given of activities which might be used to promote children's reading with some examples of checklists.

WRAY, D. (1985) *Teaching Information Skills through Project Work* (London: Hodder & Stoughton).

David Wray's book examines the structure necessary for the effective presentation of topic work, including strategies for planning, implementing and evaluating projects and some approaches for recording children's progress. These are illustrated with case studies using children in the middle years of schooling.

Reading to create

BENTON, M. and FOX, G. (1985) *Teaching Literature: Nine to Fourteen* (Oxford: Oxford University Press).

There are three parts to this book by Michael Benton and Geoff Fox:

Part 1 examines the way that readers respond to fiction in an imaginative collaboration with the author, Part 2 reviews the kinds of literature available, and in the final part some possible school policies and classroom strategies for promoting the reading of fiction are suggested.

CHAMBERS, A. (1983) *Introducing Books to Children*, London: Heinemann, 2nd edition).

In this most comprehensive account of ways of helping to create committed and enthusiastic readers, Aidan Chambers explores such issues as book provision, storytelling, reading aloud, the use of school bookshops and ways of involving authors and artists in classroom activities. There is also a section on developing response to fiction through discussion.

FRY, D. (1985) *Children Talk about Books: Seeing Themselves as Readers* (Milton Keynes: Open University Press).

This is a fascinating account of conversations with six children about their reading. The children are aged between eight and fifteen. Donald Fry also discusses why particular books and authors appeal to children, and how fiction relates to information books and films.

HAYHOE, M. and PARKER, S. (1984) *Working with Fiction* (London: Edward Arnold).

Based on work carried out with children in school, this book describes ways of encouraging children to explore literature through talk, drama, visual representations and writing. Throughout the book, Mike Hayhoe and Stephen Parker present a wealth of practical ideas with information also about resources, publications, suppliers and organisations associated with children's reading.

INGHAM, J. (1982) *Books and Reading Development* (London: Heinemann, 2nd edition).

Jennie Ingham describes the results of the Bradford Book Flood experiment in which the researchers sought to discover whether ready access to a range of books in itself improved children's reading and their appetite for books. Implications include issues concerning the arrangement and display of books, the importance of friends and family in promoting literacy and the role of head teacher and staff.

JACKSON, D. (1983) *Encounters with Books: Teaching Fiction 11–16* (London: Methuen).

David Jackson discusses what he describes as 'fresh ways of working with texts' and suggests ways of building a reading environment and developing children's response to fiction. Through case studies he describes 'phases of growth' through which children develop in their reading, with accompanying lists of reading suggestions relating to each phase.

PROTHEROUGH, R. (1983) *Developing Response to Fiction* (Milton Keynes: Open University Press).

Robert Protherough presents a series of five chapters written by secondary classroom teachers who suggest ways in which they have dealt with class readers and set books, workshop approaches and the use of short stories. In addition to these, Protherough discusses some ideas concerning children's response to story.

References

AIKEN, J. (1968) *The Wolves of Willoughby Chase* (Harmondsworth: Puffin).

ANDERSON, A. B. and STOKES, S. J. (1984) 'Social and institutional influences on the development and practice of literacy' in GOEL-MAN, H., OBERG, A. and SMITH, F. (eds) *Awakening to Literacy* (London: Heinemann).

ARNOLD, H. (1982) *Listening to Children Reading* (London: Hodder & Stoughton).

AVANN, P. (ed.) (1985) *Teaching Information Skills in the Primary School* (London: Arnold).

BEECH, J. (1985) *Learning to Read* (London: Croom Helm).

BENNETT, J. (1985) *Learning to Read with Picture Books* (third edition) (Stroud: Signal Books).

BENNETT, N., DESFORGES, C., COCKBURN, A. and WILKIN-SON, B. (1984) *The Quality of Pupil Learning Experiences* (London: Laurence Erlbaum Associates).

BENTON, M. and FOX, G. (1985) *Teaching Literature: Nine to Fourteen* (Oxford: Oxford University Press).

BETTELHEIM, B. and ZELAN, K. (1982) *On Learning to Read* (London: Thames and Hudson).

BLAUNER, R. (1964) *Alienation and Freedom* (Chicago: University of Chicago Press).

BRITTON, J. (1970) *Language and Learning* (Harmondsworth: Pelican).

BRODERICK, C. and TRUSHELL, J. (1985) 'Problems and processes: junior school pupils using word processors to produce an information leaflet' in *English in Education*, Vol 19.2.

BRONOWSKI, J. (1973) *The Ascent of Man* (London: BBC publications).

BYERS, B. (1968) *The Midnight Fox* (Harmondsworth: Puffin).

CHAMBERS, A. (1983) *Introducing Books to Children* (London: Heinemann).

CHAPMAN, J. (ed.) (1981) *The Reader and the Text* (London: Heinemann).

CHEETHAM, J. (1976) 'Quarries in the primary school' in FOX, G., HAMMOND, G., JONES, T., SMITH, F. and STERCK, K. (eds) *Writers, Critics and Children* (London: Heinemann).

CLARK, M. (1976) *Young Fluent Readers* (London: Heinemann).

CLARK, M. (1984) 'Literacy at home and at school: insights from a study of young fluent readers' in GOELMAN, H., OBERG, S. and SMITH, F. (eds) *Awakening to Literacy* (London: Heinemann).

DARCH, B. (1980) 'The Children are reading now' in *English in Education*, Vol 14.2.

DAVIES, D. (1985) 'Introducing information skills in the infant school' in AVANN, P. (ed.) *Teaching Information Skills in Primary School* (London: Arnold).

DENNIS, D. (ed.) (1984) *Meeting Children's Special Needs* (London: Heinemann).

D.E.S. (1975) *A Language for Life* (London: H.M.S.O.).

D.E.S. (1978) *Primary Education in England* (London: H.M.S.O.).

D.E.S. (1982) *Education 5–9* (London: H.M.S.O.).

D.E.S. (1983) *9–13 Middle Schools* (London: H.M.S.O.).

D.E.S. (1985) *Education 8–12 in Combined and Middle Schools* (London: H.M.S.O.).

DONALDSON, M. and REID, J. (1982) 'Language skills and reading comprehension' in HENDRY, A. (ed.) *Teaching Reading: The Key Issues* (London: Heinemann).

EWING, J. (ed.) (1985) *Reading in the New Technologies* (London: Heinemann).

FOREMAN-PECK, L. (1985) 'Evaluating children's talk about literature: a theoretical perspective' in *Children's Literature in Education*, Vol 16.4.

FOX, C. (1983) 'Talking like a book: young children's oral monologues' in MEEK, M. (ed.) *Opening Moves* (London: Institute of Education).

FOX, C. and YERRILL, K. (1983) 'The first curriculum: stories' in GILLHAM, B. (ed.) *Reading through the Curriculum* (London: Heinemann).

FOX, G. (1974) 'Travelling in time' (Editorial comment) in *Children's Literature in Education*, Vol 13.1.

FOX, G., HAMMOND, G., JONES, T., SMITH, F. and STERCK, K. (eds) (1976) *Writers, Critics and Children* (London: Heinemann).

FRANCIS, H. (1982) *Learning to Read* (London: Allen and Unwin).

FRY, D. (1985) *Children Talk About Books: Seeing Themselves as Readers* (Milton Keynes: Open University Press).

FYFE, R. and MITCHELL, E. (1985) *Reading Strategies and their Assessment* (Windsor: NFER Nelson).

GALLARD, L. (1985) 'Reading Matters' in *Ideal Home*, July 1985.

GALTON, M. and SIMON, B. (1980) *Inside the Primary Classroom* (London: Routledge & Kegan Paul).

GASKINS, I. (1981) 'Reading for learning: going beyond basals in the elementary grades' in *The Reading Teacher*, Vol 35.3.

GILLHAM, B. (ed.) (1983) *Reading through the Curriculum* (London: Heinemann).

GOELMAN, H., OBERG, S. and SMITH, F. (eds) (1984) *Awakening to Literacy* (London: Heinemann).

GOODALL, M. (1984) 'Can four year olds "read" words in the environment?' in *The Reading Teacher*, Vol 37.

HALL, N. (1985) 'When do children learn to read?' in *Reading*, Vol 19.2.

HAMBLIN, D. (1981) *Teaching Study Skills* (Oxford: Basil Blackwell).

HAYHOE, M. and PARKER, S. (1984) *Working with Fiction* (London: Arnold).

HENDRY, A. (ed.) (1982) *Teaching Reading: The Key Issues* (London: Heinemann).

HEWITT, G. (1979) 'The role of prior knowledge in reading comprehension and text response' in *Reading*, Vol 13.3.

HODGSON, J. and PRYKE, D. (1985) *A Survey of the Styles of Teaching Reading in Twenty Shropshire Primary Schools*, Shropshire L.E.A.

HOGGART, R. (1983) 'Why I value literature' in CHAMBERS, A. (1983) *Introducing Books to Children* (London: Heinemann).

HOLDAWAY, D. (1979) *The Foundations of Literacy* (London: Ashton Scholastic).

ILEA (1985) *Improving Primary Schools* (London: Inner London Education Authority).

INGHAM, J. (1982) *Books and Reading Development* (London: Heinemann).

KING, C. (1963) *Stig of the Dump* (Harmondsworth: Puffin).

KINGHAM, S. (1986) 'Using Literature to develop children's reading', (Unpublished Study for the Advanced Diploma in Language and Reading, Chester College.)

LANGER, J. (1981) 'Pre-reading plan (PReP): facilitating text comprehension' in CHAPMAN, L. J. (ed.) *The Reader and the Text* (London: Heinemann).

LAVENDER, R. (1983) 'Children using information books' in *Education 3–13*, Vol 11.1.

LUNZER, E. and GARDNER, K. (1979) *The Effective Use of Reading* (London: Heinemann).

MARTIN, T. (1986) 'Leslie: a reading failure talks about reading' in *Reading*, Vol 20.1.

MACKAY, R. and PEPIN, N. (1984) 'Children's needs in the reading curriculum' in DENNIS, D. (ed.) *Reading: Meeting Children's Special Needs* (London: Heinemann).

MAXWELL, J. (1977) *Reading Progress from 8–15* (Windsor: NFER Nelson).

McCALL, P. and PALMER, F. (1984) 'Modelling: an approach to reading comprehension' in DENNIS, D. (ed.) *Reading: Meeting Children's Special Needs* (London: Heinemann).

MEEK, M. (1982) *Learning to Read* (London: The Bodley Head).

MEEK, M. (ed.) (1983) *Opening Moves* (London: Institute of Education).

MERRITT, J. (ed.) *Reading: Today and Tomorrow* (London: University of London Press).

MOON, B. and C. (1986) *Individualised Reading* (17th edition) (Reading and Language Information Centre, University of Reading).

MOON, C. (ed.) (1985) *Practical Ways to Teach Reading* (London: Ward Lock).

MORRISON, K. (1984) 'Improving reading comprehension: approaches and practices' in *Education 3–13*, Vol 12.2.

NEVILLE, M. and PUGH, A. K. (1982) *Towards Independent Reading* (London: Heinemann).

PEARSON, H. (1984) 'Functional reading in the first school' in *Education 3–13*, Vol 12.2.

PUGH, A. K. (1978) *Silent Reading* (London: Heinemann).

PRENTICE, J. (1985) 'A personal approach to reading, using real books and involving parents' in *Reading*, Vol 19.2.

PROTHEROUGH, R. (1983) *Developing Response to Fiction* (Milton Keynes: Open University Press).

RAGGETT, M., TUTT, C. and RAGGETT, P. (eds) (1979) *Assessment and Testing of Reading* (London: Ward Lock).

ROBERTS, T. (1984) 'Real research' in *English in Education*, Vol 18.1.

ROBINSON, F. P. (1961) *Effective Study* (New York: Harper and Row).

ROBINSON, H. A. (1977) 'Comprehension: an elusive concept' in GILLILAND, J. (ed.) *Reading: Research and Classroom Practice* (London: Ward Lock).

SCHILLING, F. (1984) 'Teaching study skills in the intermediate grades' *The Reading Teacher*, Vol 37.8.

SENIOR, J. (1979) 'Reading Assessment in School' in RAGGETT, M. et al (eds) *Assessment and Testing of Reading* (London: Ward Lock).

SMITH, F. (1982a) 'What shall we teach when we teach reading?' in HENDRY, A. (ed.) *Teaching Reading: The Key Issues* (London: Heinemann).

SMITH, F. (1982b) *Writing and the Writer* (London: Heinemann).

SMITH, F. (1984) *Joining the Literacy Club* (Reading: Centre for the Teaching of Reading).

SMITH, P. (1983) *Reading Skills and Reference Work* (London: Macmillan).

SOMERFIELD, M., TORBE, M. and WARD, C. (1983) *A Framework for Reading* (London: Heinemann).

SOUTHGATE, V. (1984) *Reading: Teaching for Learning* (London: Macmillan).

SOUTHGATE, V., ARNOLD, H. and JOHNSON, S. (1981) *Extending Beginning Reading* (London: Heinemann).

STRANG, R. (1972) 'Sequential aspects of reading development' in MELNIK, A. and MERRITT, J. (eds) *Reading: Today and Tomorrow* (London: University of London Press).

TEALE, W. H. (1984) 'Reading to young children: its significance for literacy development' in GOELMAN, H., OBERG, S. and SMITH, F. (eds) *Awakening to Literacy* (London: Heinemann).

TIZARD, B. and HUGHES, M. (1984) *Young Children Learning* (London: Fontana).

TONJES, M. (1980) 'Adaptable rates and strategies for efficient comprehension in the effective reader' in BRAY, G. and PUGH, T. (eds) *The Reading Connection* (London: Ward Lock).

TOPPING, K. (1984) 'Paired reading' in *Child Education*, Dec. 1984.

TRELEASE, J. (1984) *The Read-Aloud Handbook* (Harmondsworth: Penguin).

WADE, B. and CHERRINGTON, J. (1985) 'Talk towards text making: making an information book' in *Education 3–13*, Vol 13.1.

WATERLAND, L. (1985) *Read with Me* (Stroud: The Thimble Press).

WELLS, G. (1982) *Story reading and the Development of Symbolic Skills* (Bristol University, Centre for the Study of Language and Communication).

WILSON, J. and GUNNING, D. (1983) 'Catering for a range of abilities in topic work' in *Education 3–13*, Vol 11.2.

WRAY, D. (1982) 'Research insights into extending reading' in *Reading*, Vol 16.1.

WRAY, D. (1985) *Teaching Information Skills through Project Work* (London: Hodder & Stoughton).

Index

the last date